'As leaders in sustainability, we are expected to have many skills–be great communicators, collaborators, influencers, storytellers and systems thinkers, all while being self-aware, agile, adaptive, accountable, passionate, persistent, resilient and authentic. The list can be overwhelming.

The beauty of this book is its simplicity and practicality. Ingrid's 'wise leadership' model provides a framework accompanied by tips and tools to hone these skills for both emerging and well-established sustainability leaders at a time when this style of leadership is more important than ever.

Ingrid's personal journey of resilience not only enables her to contextualise this style of leadership, but apply her learnings and experience so we can be more effective in our own path to becoming 'naturally successful wise leaders'.

I wish I'd had a copy of this book earlier in my career; it certainly would be treasured and well-thumbed!'

PAOLO BEVILACQUA, GENERAL MANAGER -
REAL UTILITIES, FRASERS PROPERTY AUSTRALIA

'If ever there was a time to tap into the collective wisdom of previous generations across all cultures, it is now. Ingrid has travelled extensively, read broadly and listened openly. Now she has synthesised her wisdom into a comprehensive and easy to understand book. This is a guide for all those who aspire to be more successful leaders, who work with the grain of nature, not against it.'

JULIAN CRAWFORD, DIRECTOR,
BLUE MOUNTAINS WORLD HERITAGE INSTITUTE

'Working in sustainability is draining. Every day you read more sad facts about the state of the world.

But changing the world is a marathon, not a sprint. You need strength, resilience, stamina, persistence. It takes courage, resolve, confidence and great integrity to do hard things, to do the right thing. You will get frustrated, angry, upset. Because sustainability is not everyone's first priority. But if you are patient, professional, collaborative and respectful of others, you will have a positive impact.

This book teaches us many things: the importance of having a growth mindset; how to gain satisfaction through both achieving bold goals and creating incremental change; how to recognise the dire state of Earth's life support systems while finding hope in things you can control and influence; how to develop meaningful relationships with stakeholders so that they become allies; the importance of spending time in nature.

Ingrid Messner's work has been useful to me and several of my team members in the successful development of our 2030 Sustainability Strategy. I think that many of the ideas in this book can help sustainability professionals be more content and healthier as we struggle to influence others and deliver positive environmental outcomes.'

CHRIS NUNN, HEAD OF SUSTAINABILITY &
PLATFORM OPERATIONS I REAL ESTATE, AMP CAPITAL

"Naturally Successful' directly addresses the challenges faced by climate and sustainability leaders, including complexity, overwhelm and grief. Ingrid Messner draws on traditional wisdom and business excellence to guide the reader through the steps required to become a more effective and impactful leader. As *'Naturally Successful'* explains, we have the solutions we need, and this book will help more leaders build an environmentally sustainable, socially just and economically viable world.'

URSULA HOGBEN BSC LLB MLM - FOUNDER, CORPORATE
LAWYER, DIRECTOR & ADVISOR OF SUSTAINABLE COMPANIES

'*Naturally Successful* is a thought-provoking read for leaders, aspiring leaders, or anyone curious on how to create a more abundant life of purpose. Ingrid has packed Naturally Successful with such insight and wisdom that it is one of those books that you will just want to keep coming back to.'

ALAN RIVA, GUIDE & ADVISOR: LIVING, LEADING & GROWING THROUGH PRESENCE & PURPOSE

"*Naturally Successful*' is an absolute godsend in a time of re-assessing how we can best lead our businesses and, most importantly, our people. This thought-provoking book shows us how we can be phenomenal leaders and have maximum impact, while also enhancing our natural energy sources and looking after ourselves. It's a game-changer!'

VICTORIA BLACK, MULTI-AWARD-WINNING ENTREPRENEUR WINNER AUSTRALIAN BUSINESSWOMAN OF THE YEAR (OPTUS/MYBUSINESS AWARDS 2016) WINNER AUSTRALIAN START-UP BUSINESS OF THE YEAR 2018

'This moment in our history as a species is loaded with immense challenges, but they are not insurmountable and in fact there is great hope. Humble and harmonic leadership, rooted in nature's wisdom, will set the foundation for more harmonic actions to protect our planet for future generations.

Ingrid has practised opening this wisdom for me, my team and many others in her journey. She's now crystallised this wisdom into the book (printed on a gift from our Earth) you now hold in your hands. Treat this book wisely and with love as you would treat your mother. In doing so, we create greater hope in a sustainable and just future for all.'

MIKEY LEUNG, CO-CREATOR / COFOUNDER / DIRECTOR, DIGITAL STORYTELLERS – STORIES FOR IMPACT

'I found it quite topical reading this book this week. On Monday I got asked to take on additional responsibilities for a large transformational project and whilst there is a significant chunk of systems change, the bigger and more challenging part is the required change in people's mindset, so everything written in this book is completely relevant!

Many of the leadership ideas and concepts in this book might not be radical or new, but Ingrid has been able to pull them all together in a clear & cohesive way and I found her way of bringing in examples from nature very relevant and meaningful.

For me the one key learning is that we all have to slow down to speed up.'

RACHEL ANDERSON, HEAD OF SHARED SERVICES

NATURALLY SUCCESSFUL

NATURALLY SUCCESSFUL

HOW WISE LEADERS MANAGE THEIR ENERGY, INFLUENCE OTHERS AND CREATE POSITIVE IMPACT

INGRID MESSNER

Naturally Successful
Copyright © 2021 by Ingrid Messner.
All rights reserved.

Published by Grammar Factory Publishing, an imprint of MacMillan Company Limited.

Grammar Factory Publishing
MacMillan Company Limited
25 Telegram Mews, 39th Floor, Suite 3906
Toronto, Ontario, Canada
M5V 3Z1

www.grammarfactory.com

Messner, Ingrid,
    Naturally Successful: How wise leaders manager their energy, influence others and create positive impact / Ingrid Messner

Paperback ISBN 978-1-989737-20-0
eBook ISBN 978-1-989737-21-7

1. BUS071000 Business & Economics / Leadership 2. SEL027000 Self-Help / Personal Growth / Success. 3.BUS072000 Business & Economics / Development / Sustainable Development.

Production Credits
Cover design by Designerbility
Interior layout design by Dania Zafar
Graphs and illustrations by Sam Boyle
Book production and editorial services by Grammar Factory Publishing

Grammar Factory's Carbon Neutral Publishing Commitment
From January 1st, 2020 onwards, Grammar Factory Publishing is proud to be neutralizing the carbon footprint of all printed copies of its authors' books printed by or ordered directly through Grammar Factory or its affiliated companies through the purchase of Gold Standard-Certified International Offsets.

Disclaimer
The material in this publication is of the nature of general comment only and does not represent professional advice. It is not intended to provide specific guidance for particular circumstances, and it should not be relied on as the basis for any decision to take action or not take action on any matter which it covers. Readers should obtain professional advice where appropriate, before making any such decision. To the maximum extent permitted by law, the author and publisher disclaim all responsibility and liability to any person, arising directly or indirectly from any person taking or not taking action based on the information in this publication.

Aboriginal and Torres Strait Islander people should be aware that this book may contain images or names of people now deceased.

*This book is dedicated
to my sons Timo and Leon Schmechel...*

*and the next seven generations who will live
on this precious, beautiful and magical planet Earth.*

*My hope is that this book inspires and supports leaders
to connect with, care for and commit to a healthy planet
with more ease and joy.*

CONTENTS

ABOUT THE AUTHOR

Ingrid Messner leverages timeless wisdom to optimise performance and wellbeing. She supports leaders to better manage their energy, enabling them to develop greater influence and impact.

Ingrid is a leadership expert with over twenty-five years' experience working with clients from diverse countries, cultures and industries.

Her portfolio includes roles in corporate and management consultancy and running leadership programs and wilderness retreats, and she has accreditation as an executive coach as well as an MBA.

Her business acumen, deep connection to nature, and firsthand insight into over fifty cultures worldwide provide an innovative approach to success.

She creates stimulating spaces that inspire leaders to discover new ways to be, think and do. They are equipped to thrive sustainably, achieve goals effortlessly and become naturally successful.

Ingrid was born in Germany and moved with her family to Sydney, Australia, in 2004. When she is not coaching, mentoring or facilitating, she can be found somewhere in nature — bushwalking, camping, hiking or meditating.

At the heart of everything Ingrid does is a fundamental belief that healthy people need a healthy planet. Our connection to nature is unbreakable — we are part of the same system. A fact that is, unfortunately, too often overlooked in today's economies and society. Ingrid works with people who want to change this and create services and products that have a positive impact on humanity and planet.

ACKNOWLEDGEMENTS AND GRATITUDE

Writing this book often felt like a big and daring adventure.

As many of my insights and the wisdom I am sharing came from Indigenous people and nature, I would like to first acknowledge that most of my work for this book took place on the land of the First Nation people Gayamaygal and Dharug, the traditional custodians of the areas around Sydney's Northern Beaches (and beyond). I'd like to pay my respect to their Elders, past, present and emerging.

I would not have got the book across the finish line without the support and encouragement of countless people. I'd like to thank everyone who inspired me, challenged my thinking, taught me valuable lessons along the way, allowed the space for new insights to emerge, took me on walks and hikes to clear my head, shared a glass of wine or bubbles to celebrate milestones, or just listened to me sharing 'idea bombs'.

There is no way to name all who have been involved, but I do want to acknowledge a few by name.

For the book content:

I am very grateful to the people who helped me understand Indigenous / First Nations cultures and their relevance for leaders today: Susan Moylan-Coombs, Max Dulumunmun Harrison, Bob Randall, Djalu Gurruwiwi and many more in Australia, Africa and North America.

My connection to nature changed after I spent some time in the wild with John P Milton, Tom Brown Jr and Malcolm Ringwalt. Carmen Morales offered me a female and South American perspective.

Many of my practical insights on mindfulness and meditation came from SN Goenka, my Vipassana meditation teacher, and John P Milton, who taught us a variety of mindfulness techniques at Way of Nature retreats.

Meetings with Peter Senge and Dr Ha Vinh Tho in Bhutan at the Gross National Happiness Centre, workshops with the Presencing Institute/ ULab and with Sarah Cornally helped me to understand systems from many different angles.

Thought Leaders Business School (founded by Matt Church and Peter Cook) connected me with many brilliant mentors and the most supportive peer community I have ever met. A lot of thinking that appeared in this book was challenged and clarified by this community.

A big thank you to my clients (whose names I have changed in the stories to guarantee privacy) and business leaders like Leila Fourie, Stephen Choi, Chris Nunn, Binowee Bayles and several others who shared their insights with me during the writing process.

For the process of writing this book:

Kelly Irving, thank you for guiding me perfectly through the whole writing process. Your structure, feedback, editing, encouragement and professionalism made this book possible. You were the best book coach I could have hoped for.

Thank you to Scott MacMillan and the whole Grammar Factory team for making the editing, design and publishing process so easy, seamless and professional.

I am grateful to YuDan Shi, Ella Zhang, Julian Crawford and Jürgen Schmechel, who patiently worked their way through my first draft manuscript and offered some invaluable feedback.

For supporting me while writing:

I discovered that being an author is an emotional roller coaster. My best friend and husband of twenty-seven years, Jürgen Schmechel, needs a special award for always having my back and discussing all my ideas and challenges. You are the best! Thank you to my sons Timo and Leon, for just being you and for keeping me grounded and connected to the next generation.

Thank you to my hiking buddies at WildWomen, especially Di Westaway, Ann Jenkins, Kate Clissold, and my Coastrek Team, Katrina, Heather, Julie, Jenny and Ilda. You made sure that I relearned to walk and talk simultaneously — eventually finding my balance and energy again.

Thank you also to Lewis McLean, my exercise physiologist at The CUBE Gym who helped me to learn walking again — twice.

There were also several friends in Australia and Germany who spent countless hours on the phone with me — helping me to stay energised and clear. A special thank you to Anja, Tatjana, Wiebke, Franziska, YuDan and Ella.

Finally, last but not least...

Thank you to you, the reader. Thank you for picking up this book, which I've written with you in mind. My hope for you is that you become truly naturally successful. A wise leader who feels energised, influential and impactful.

INTRODUCTION

Dave is a respected and successful leader in the sustainability space. Lately, he is struggling to keep his mojo up and stay positive.

The other day, he shared on LinkedIn another article on the impacts of climate change. The week before, he posted something on biodiversity and solutions to reduce plastic waste. The scientific facts are shocking. His frustration about insufficient action to counterbalance the developments is boiling. Even though his organisation has an award-winning sustainability strategy, he often faces resistance from internal and external stakeholders who just don't want to understand that they need to do more. Some even ignore him and his team.

After following media coverage on the most recent natural disaster, he noticed that he has started to feel a bit hopeless and no longer sure whether the worst-case scenarios can be averted. He has to make a conscious effort not to let this impact his mood and work. He knows that his team, his community and his family are counting on him to deliver positive change. He wants to be a beacon of hope and inspire more action but often feels exhausted, like he's not doing enough and is running into walls. His stress levels are quite high, and he has a few nights when he does not sleep well.

There are so many projects on his always growing task list that there is hardly any time for him to recharge and connect with family and friends. Whenever he finds a moment, he is also tirelessly working on making his and his family's lifestyle more sustainable. He is keen to get out into nature with his friends and notices that, when he finds the time, he comes back feeling a lot better. But, unfortunately, this is happening less and less.

Dave knows something has to change but is not sure how to go about making this change.

FACING THE MESS WE ARE IN ...
IT IS EXHAUSTING

How about you? Are you exhausted by trying to stay positive? Do you feel like you're working an uphill battle against an avalanche of growing tasks? Are you often confronted with difficult people and other blockages that slow down your projects? Are you frustrated because you are not seeing positive impact and results quickly enough?

Your set of challenges might be unique, yet, you might be sharing some elements of these with your fellow leaders. There is a high chance that your performance (and wellbeing) is impacted by one or more of the following four problems:

1. *Too much stress*, which causes a loss of energy.

2. *Frustration with difficult people*, which limits your potential to influence.

3. *Overwhelm*, which leads to inconsistent impact and results.

4. *Loss of connection to nature*, which leaves you feeling empty and stressed.

It's likely that you're very passionate about planet and people and want to make a positive difference — *now*.

But you're doing this in a world that is VUCA: volatile, uncertain, complex and ambiguous. Alarming language like 'climate emergency', 'water scarcity', 'system break-down' and 'species extinction' only increases your sense of urgency and impacts who you are when you do your work.

This perceived speed of change subconsciously triggers your sense of safety — an innate human need. We are constantly playing catch up. External sources, like science and media, constantly tell us that the world is changing — and not for the better. Our bodies unintentionally and automatically go into fight/flight response, stress levels rise, and high-level cognitive functioning becomes impaired. The risk of burning out becomes real for many. High urgency causes us to constantly sprint, even though we know that the challenge is a marathon race. Performance and wellbeing suffer.

Leaders experience challenge overload and often over-commit themselves.

A long list of projects with big, complex and urgent tasks often produces a sense of overwhelm that cannot be managed just by increasing personal productivity.

Yes, there is too much to do in too little time. However, often, our effectiveness is defined more by how we show up than what we actually do. How much positive, personal energy can you bring to the challenge?

Sustainability is such a diverse topic that leaders have to deal with a variety of different stakeholders — quite a few of those might be labelled 'difficult' and may not even care about the cause. Clashing world views and mindsets are encountered daily. It often feels exhausting and stressful to influence all of those stakeholders towards positive change. Getting everyone on your side and working as a cohesive whole is a challenging leadership task. Energy levels are easily drained when people resist. How can you deal effectively with 'difficult' people?

With increased stress and less energy to implement solutions in a patient and persistent way, your point of view as leader sometimes narrows to the most immediate issues at hand. Awareness is limited and influences from a variety of systems go unnoticed. The big picture and system view get lost. How can you get aligned with the natural energy flow of the surrounding systems and not work against them?

Something similar can be observed in today's business and society. The lack of nature-connection awareness and capabilities adds another aspect to your leadership challenges that not many leaders consider and know how to deal with.

Disruptive technologies easily give us the impression that these developments are more important today than natural processes. They are fast-paced and high-energy and, thus, place stress and a sense of urgency on many leaders. At the same time, increased nature connection could be the antidote.

However, many people have lost the intimate connection to nature — the very thing that nourishes us, provides us with a habitat and home, and effortlessly organises life based on timeless principles and rules.

Right now, you often don't have the energy to show up as your best possible self. You don't always know how to be a wise and effective leader.

IT'S NOT ALL DOOM AND GLOOM: YOU CAN RE-LEARN WISE LEADERSHIP!

If you are a leader who is keen to create more positive impact while suffering less stress, it is time to remember some timeless truths. In some ways, it is literally going back to basic human wisdom and the laws of nature. Technology and science can be supporting elements but are not necessary to become naturally successful.

A renewed, holistic perspective on how to lead yourself, others and a system wisely will give you the energy to create more positive impact with less stress.

To become naturally successful, you will need to tackle the problems described above. To do this, it is important to put equal importance on leading both yourself and others in an effective and energising way while being highly aware of and connected to your context — the systems that you and your stakeholders are part of.

I call this type of leadership 'Wise Leadership'. It makes you naturally successful.

A while ago, we knew how to lead in this way, but then it was forgotten. We have to re-learn it.

As a wise leader, you develop a full system perspective for all situations. By bringing self, stakeholders and systems together, you align these forces, create flow and become naturally successful. A stakeholder is someone who is important for the success of your work or life. A system is an assemblage or combination of things, people or parts forming a complex or unitary whole. By leading this way, you achieve more with less effort. The graphic below shows how it all fits together.

THE WISE LEADERSHIP UNIVERSE

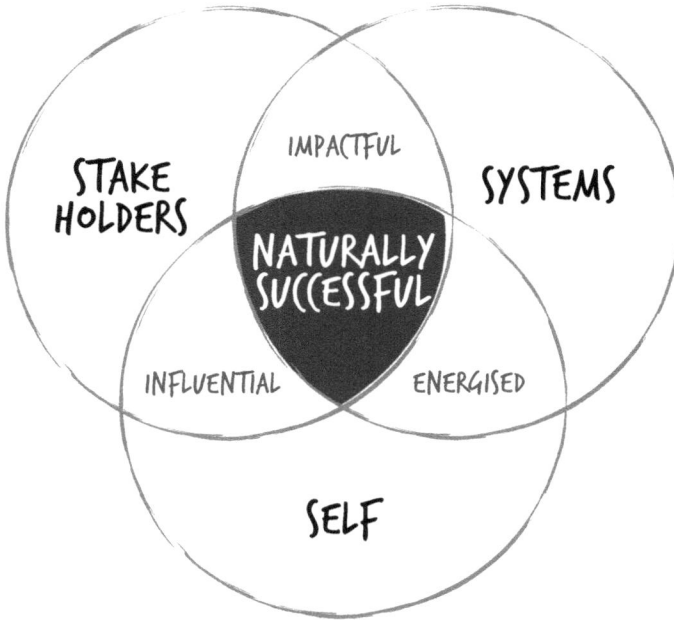

It all starts with your SELF. Being aware of what is going on in your body, mind, emotions and spirit — at any moment throughout the day — has to be your top priority. Your energy levels need care and management. Everyone knows that you can only give what you have got. And yet, even though it sounds simple, it is not easy. It becomes doable once you get a better understanding of how nature and human bodies work together. To upgrade your mindset is just one element of this.

Once you have taken care of yourself, you are ready to take on the world outside of you: other people. Even though your STAKEHOLD-ERS often have roles with fancy titles, they are first and foremost human beings. Deeply understanding how another person ticks, what motivates them and what will make them change their course of action only happens when you take the time to listen deeply and with the right intent. Communication and collaboration cannot be rushed and forced. You cannot create positive impact alone. It is a collaborative effort.

All of your work (and life) happens in a variety of SYSTEMS. All systems operate based on similar principles and rules. System awareness affects the success of your leadership. Understanding context and important connections in a system supports you to find an effective focus on relevant details. Change happens when you manage to tap into the right flow of energy and not swim against the currents.

Wise leaders in the 21st century take care of themselves, create common ground with stakeholders and work with and within the web of life systems.

Leading this way makes you naturally successful: a state where your wellbeing has moved from stressed to energised, your reputation has evolved from insignificant to influential, and your performance has developed from overwhelmed to impactful.

How does this sound to you?

And how do I know all of this?

WHY I WROTE THIS BOOK

I have seen way too many people, who want to create a better world, unnecessarily struggle their way through work and life. For many years I was one of them. I was largely unaware of the simple solutions that are available to all of us and all around us. But I have now learned those solutions, and I want to share them.

I have worked in and with large organisations with global supply chains. I have travelled in more than fifty countries, and often seen the other end of corporate influence: poor working conditions, increased waste, destruction of nature. I have also seen the many benefits that these economic activities bring to people in other countries.

I have learned that what is good and what is bad is never clear cut. There are always many different perspectives and nuances. This makes it complicated for leaders in the sustainability and social change space. For more than thirty years, I have led, mentored, coached and facilitated leaders who are keen to increase their positive impact and make the world a better place. I have seen many of them thrive, struggle, burn out and bounce back again — always driven by an inspiring passion for their cause.

Over the last fifteen-plus years I have spent a lot of time outdoors, often somewhere wild and remote, meditating on my own. I have realised that most people are no longer aware of our deep connection to nature. I have also observed, with myself and many of my clients, that we are no longer aware of how our bodies and minds need nature to thrive.

During the last three years, I had to overcome two separate and very different health issues that both required learning to walk again. Badly breaking my tibia plateau (the weight-bearing part of the knee) and dealing with a viral infection of my vestibular system (part of the balance system, which affects brain function) has been an emotional, life-changing roller coaster. My patience, resilience and resourcefulness all increased exponentially — and involuntarily. I got very frustrated with the health care system treating the body as many separate parts. This frustration helped me to become a largely self-taught expert on integrative self-care, nutrition, brain health, and the power of exercise and nature connection.

In addition, a variety of Indigenous people and Elders taught me how their timeless wisdom can support us in our busy lives and in today's business world. Their wisdom has changed my perspective on life significantly, and I am hugely grateful for what they have shared with me.

Bringing all of these knowledge systems (business, nature, other cultures, health and wellbeing) together has become a bit of a quest for me. Given my unique combination of interests and lived experiences, I have been able to create safe and inspiring spaces for people to have conversations where they explore different ways of being, thinking and doing.

People and nature are suffering. I believe the world needs more leaders who work effectively towards an environmentally sustainable, socially just and economically viable and inclusive world. We have all the solutions we need. What is missing is the will and skill of more leaders to step up and implement these solutions. We need leaders who are deeply connected to nature, other people and themselves. Leaders who are naturally successful human beings because they connect, care and commit themselves to change our world for the better. This is a big task and a daunting journey.

This book contains some of my discoveries and insights that might be helpful for you in your quest to grow as a leader — having more positive impact while experiencing less stress.

In this book I have created a roadmap to help you navigate the Wise Leadership Universe. This roadmap integrates the three spheres of the Wise Leadership Universe described above (Self, Stakeholders, Systems) with the three key practices that a wise leader focuses on every day. Those three practices are to:

Connect

You are always aware that you have to lead your SELF and others (your STAKEHOLDERS) and that you are operating in a specific context (a variety of SYSTEMS). You have awareness of what is happening in and around you. You observe it in a calm way, with curiosity and compassion. By accepting what is, you are able to pinpoint challenges and their causes. Accepting something does not mean that you condone it. You are just noticing a reality. You also appreciate what is good and working already. **Connect is all about awareness.**

Care

You deeply care for people and planet — and all beings in nature. You approach all leadership tasks with a sense of care. You have the courage to be vulnerable and kind. You align your vision, values and purpose with new insights and decide on your next action steps. **Care is all about action.**

Commit

You take full personal responsibility to create positive, win-win results and changes. You are spreading hope and aim for positive impact. You implement your action and accountability plan. When needed, you are flexible enough to adapt your plans. Your learning from this increases your awareness and connection. **Commit is all about accountability and delivering results.**

Connect, care, commit is a circular learning and leadership process. It is neither linear nor does it have an end. It is needed for all levels of leadership: leading yourself, leading others and leading in a system.

When these three practices are combined with the three spheres of the Wise Leadership Universe, we have:

THE WISE LEADER'S SKILLS MAP

	CONNECT	CARE	COMMIT
SELF	SELF AWARENESS	ENERGY MANAGEMENT	ACCOUNTABILTY
STAKEHOLDERS	COMMUNICATION	COLLABORATION	INFLUENCE
SYSTEMS	CONTEXT AWARENESS	STEWARDSHIP	IMPACT

The Wise Leader's Skills Map guides you to become a wise leader who is naturally successful. In the coming pages I explore the key skills in each leadership area, how you can apply them and what their benefits might be for you and for others.

HOW TO USE THIS BOOK

The nine areas in the Wise Leader's Skill Map above represent the key leadership skills you need to connect, care and commit at each level of leadership. Use this map and the following explanations to navigate to your topics of special interest or to zoom out to see how they all fit together and complement each other. Practise all of them together and you will become more and more naturally successful.

This book is structured to correspond to the nine leadership skills in the map. Part 1, represented by the upper row, is all about self. Part 2, represented by the middle row, focuses on stakeholders. Part 3, or the bottom row, is about leading in systems. The three chapters in each part of the book discuss the three skills in each row in more detail.

Here is what you can expect to find in each chapter:

Part 1 — SELF: You can only give what you have got

1. Self-Awareness: Notice your state
Becoming highly aware of what is happening within you and how you are connecting to other people and the environment is the foundation for your leadership. This chapter looks at different processes and tools that offer you fresh perspectives on where to reduce stress and what to change to become more effective.

2. Energy Management: Prioritise your self-care
We all know that we have to put our own oxygen mask on first, and yet we often do not practise proper self-care. This chapter offers you a holistic way of managing your energy levels so that you can show up as your best self.

3. Accountability: Create energy for change
Things only get better when you feel 100 per cent responsible for achieving a specific outcome. You are the only person responsible for your own energy levels. You can't lead others until you lead yourself. This chapter invites you to explore all success factors that make accountability effective.

Part 2 — STAKEHOLDERS: Influence and activate the best

4. Communication: Get to know each other
Meaningful and trusting relationships with other people are the foundation for effective collaboration and influence. How aware are you of what is going on for another person? Shortcuts make

things 'difficult'. This chapter describes the elements of effective communication.

5. Collaboration: Work together

Big challenges can only be solved when people work together in ways that cause less friction and more flow. This chapter defines the five core elements of collaboration that need your consideration.

6. Influence: Commit to win for all

Working with your stakeholders means that you won't have the authority to tell them what to do or change. All you can do is influence their perspectives and behaviours. This chapter offers a snapshot of the psychology of behaviour change and how you can influence your stakeholders.

Part 3 — SYSTEMS: Let context be your guide

7. Context-Awareness: Sense the whole system

Everything is connected and influencing your results. How much of what is impacting you and others do you notice on a daily basis? This chapter provides many different perspectives and tools to explore your reality in new and more effective ways.

8. Stewardship: Care about and for the system

By approaching all people and environments around you with a sense of care, you become a force for good and a strategic influencer. This chapter offers a brief description of the seven universal principles that drive our life and work. It also describes how a steward can be effective.

9. Impact: Define what success is

Every leadership action has an impact. There are different types and ways of looking at these. This chapter explores how success can be defined and how you can relate to it to become naturally successful.

By practising all of the nine Wise Leadership skills, you will move from surviving to thriving.

You become a pro at being fully aligned with and supported by nature. You learn how to have clarity and focus on the right things at the right time. It becomes easier to activate the right people to support your cause and projects. You achieve more with less stress. Watch your positive impact and legacy grow.

You will feel energised, influential and impactful — in short: naturally successful.

Are you ready to explore the pathways to new levels of success?

Let's dive in.

PART 1

SELF

YOU CAN ONLY GIVE
WHAT YOU HAVE GOT

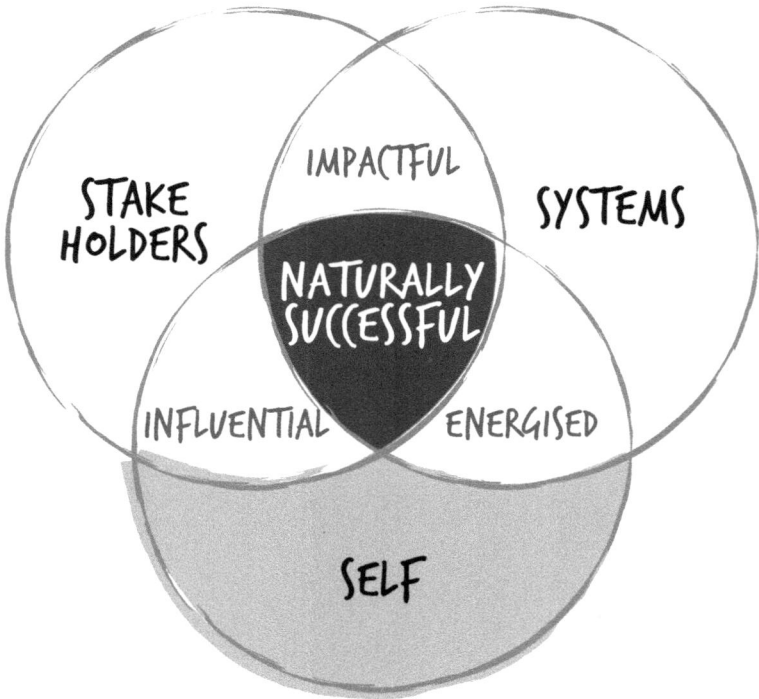

Wise Leadership starts with your SELF. Leading yourself well is the foundation to becoming naturally successful. It prevents you from feeling exhausted, overwhelmed and frustrated.

Everyone knows the simple fact that you can only give what you have got. And yet, even though it sounds simple, it is not easy. It becomes doable once you get a better understanding of how nature and human bodies work together. To upgrade your mindset is one important element of this.

In the following three chapters, you can expect to learn how to:

- CONNECT more intensely with your SELF by increasing your self-awareness;

- CARE more for your SELF by improving your personal energy management; and

- COMMIT to your SELF by demonstrating accountability and actually implementing your self-care activities.

We often feel that self-care is selfish, when it is actually a service to the people around you. No one likes a tired, grumpy and chaotic leader. The more energy you have, the more you can give to others and your causes.

An unknown source described it vividly:

> 'An empty lantern provides no light. Self-care is the fuel that allows your light to shine brightly.'

CHAPTER 1

SELF-AWARENESS: NOTICE YOUR STATE

Knowing yourself is the beginning of all wisdom.

ARISTOTLE

	CONNECT	CARE	COMMIT
SELF	SELF AWARENESS	ENERGY MANAGEMENT	ACCOUNTABILTY
STAKEHOLDERS	COMMUNICATION	COLLABORATION	INFLUENCE
SYSTEMS	CONTEXT AWARENESS	STEWARDSHIP	IMPACT

Julia enters the room where I have been waiting for her to turn up to our coaching session. She is ten minutes late. Everything around her feels a bit rushed and stressed. She notices that she has forgotten to bring her notes and rushes out of the room again. Returning five minutes later, she tries to smile and says, 'Now, we can start…'

Julia works in a medium-sized business in the area of social sustainability. She is very passionate about her area of work as she can clearly see the changes that some of her projects deliver for other people that she deeply cares about.

The CEO has given her a massive project on top of her normal work. He is expecting her to deliver the project in a few months' time. Her support resources are not yet clearly defined, but she has already started to work on the project by recruiting team members and outlining a project plan.

Meanwhile, at home, her relationship with her partner starts to fall apart. He has his own challenges at work and in his personal life. Julia and her partner constantly clash on even the tiniest things. Most of the time, Julia is now the one taking care of their two small children. This volatile home situation comes with its own challenges. There is no space and time for her to relax and recharge. She has so many things on her to-do list that she hardly gets any decent sleep. She only sleeps about four or five hours a night and is often awake worrying about the future.

Recently, her health has started to deteriorate. A persistent cough and sore throat won't go away. Her shoulders and back hurt and she is gaining weight. All of this makes her very unhappy and often unproductive.

'I just don't have time to look after myself,' she exclaims. She explains that the new project — if delivered well — will not only build trust and increase her reputation with her boss and the CEO, it will also give her valuable exposure in the company and the industry. It is an important stepping stone for her next career move. Her head is spinning … where should she start and how can she best get through this?

Does all this sound familiar?

> *It's important not just to survive this madness, but to grow as a leader and come out on the other side thriving.*

Over the course of a few months, I helped Julia to reflect on what was really important to her. By growing her awareness of what was going on in all areas of her life and how these events were impacting each other, she realised that energy management would be much more important for her than focusing on productivity and time management. She also started to see what was already working in her life and where her strengths were at work. By appreciating and accepting her situation more fully, she was able to align her day-to-day actions with her overall, bigger goals and KPIs. I supported her to develop an action plan and held her accountable. During our fortnightly check-in calls, we discussed her recent learnings and adapted her action plan on an ongoing basis.

After a short time, Julia started to feel tiny improvements in her energy levels and her health improved. It became easier for her to decide what mattered most in every moment. She got a lot better at setting boundaries and respectfully saying no to demands. We kept working together and, in the end, she successfully delivered the project, received very positive feedback from all sides, and her relationship with her partner improved as well.

In order to grow and thrive as a leader,
you first have to make yourself a priority.

TAKING A MACRO VIEW

One of the main challenges in our busy, fast-paced world is slowing down and stepping out of the hamster wheel of our unconscious routines. Achieving better self-awareness is like the difference between running and walking through a beautiful landscape: things just pass by when you run, but when you walk slowly and consciously you discover some amazing, new details. Think of it like a quick-cut GoPro video versus a carefully taken macro photo. What offers you a better chance of experiencing new insights?

When you are not slowing down and are not fully aware, you might already be experiencing too much stress. This might be causing you to lose energy and mojo without noticing your precarious state. But even if *you* do not notice — other people will.

This idea of slowing down and becoming aware may seem to contradict some of our strongly held beliefs on how to become successful today.

We still believe that we have to DO a lot —
instead of BE a lot.

You might feel an overall sense of overwhelm without being able to identify exactly what causes the energy-draining feeling. Once you manage to calm your mind to a certain degree, the causes of the overwhelm often become obvious and tackling them becomes much easier. Your mindset and thinking often create too many unrealistic expectations and put pressure on you. This leads to taking on too much in order to maintain the image of being an in-control overachiever who makes things perfect. This leads to inconsistent results, which, in turn, makes you put in even more effort instead of stepping out and noticing what is going on.

Psychologist Carl Jung said, 'Until you make the unconscious conscious, it will direct your life and you will call it fate.'

Increasing your self-awareness gives you the
opportunity to pause a moment, and then decide
more pro-actively how to respond instead of
automatically reacting without thinking.

You are aware of your actions and, thus, more in control of how you show up in the world. This approach focuses very much on you as an individual. Some parts of society and the business community still see slowing down and reflecting as 'navel gazing'. Most people just start to reflect in moments of crisis. However, there is more and more evidence that soft skills determine success more than hard skills.

A study on 'What Predicts Executive Success?' was conducted by a research team at Cornell University's School of Industrial and Labor Relations. They studied seventy-two executives at public and private companies in the USA (revenues from $50 million to $5 billion). The result: a high self-awareness score was the strongest predictor of overall success.

Harvard psychologists Matthew A Killingsworth and Daniel T Gilbert used a special 'track your happiness' iPhone app to conduct research on what people were doing at specific moments and how this made them feel. The results: 'We spend at least half our time thinking about something other than our immediate surroundings, and most of this daydreaming doesn't make us happy.'

With the challenges around us increasing all the time, it becomes even more important to actively work on one's self-awareness — now.

Self-awareness is the first step to managing your energy levels and, thus, becomes the basis for everything else.

KNOW THYSELF

Self-awareness is an awareness of your internal world (body, mind, emotions, spirit) and how you connect to the outside world of other people and environments.

From the Ancient Greek term 'know thyself' to contemporary Western psychology, the topic of self-awareness has been studied widely by philosophers, artists and many different types of scientists. Their definitions vary in nuance. Before the Ancient Greeks, the Buddha and Indigenous people had their own versions of the concept. Improving one's self-awareness is a timeless quest that is even more relevant today, but it is often seen as a passive capability that a leader either has or hasn't. That is an unhelpful point of view. Actively improving your self-awareness will allow you to pinpoint the areas in your life that stand between you and your success and overall wellbeing.

As a leader, it is crucial that you notice what is happening in you, for you, with you and around you at any given moment — with an open mind and without judgement. Self-awareness is the result of the process of observing sensations in your body, noticing any emotions and thoughts that come up, knowing what mindset you are acting from, feeling your current location in space and sensing any influences from the environment. It is the complex skill of analysing your energy levels and knowing exactly what state you are in. Your senses play an important role in all of these activities.

Nowadays, we live in a world of sensory overwhelm, mainly caused by increasing urbanisation (city noises, visual and tactile overload in shopping malls, and 24/7 media). There is less silence and space. To survive, we have started to filter incoming sensory stimuli and numb our senses. This leads to missing out on a lot of subtle but important data from our environments and our bodies. We no longer notice the finer details. This becomes very obvious once you spend a few days on your own in nature. Your senses sharpen again, and you will notice a lot more detail. Coming back to a city after this relaxing and clarifying time can be quite shocking.

Self-awareness can be achieved with four key practices:

1. Mindfulness: Observing your current state
2. Journaling: Discovering new insights
3. Gathering Feedback: Considering external views
4. Energy Mapping: Visualising your current state

Let's explore each.

1. Mindfulness: Observing your current state

Nowadays, mindfulness is a well-known concept, and yet it is still often misunderstood or not fully accepted. In its purest forms, it is more than just paying attention to what is in the present moment; you need to observe your body sensations at the same time — without judgement. I see it as a kind of gym for your brain: You learn to train your mind's muscles not to immediately react to any positive or negative events or situations. As with working out at the gym, if you want to see results you need to put in a lot of practice — and boring repetitions. With mindfulness, you train your skills of slowing down, pausing, being patient, resting, reflecting, acceptance, kindness, compassion, empathy and a few more.

Mindfulness helps you to realise where the cracks in your overwhelming and stressful life are. It allows you to pinpoint where stress comes from.

Visualise your body and mind as having many, many small receptors where you can receive energy and send out energy to other people and the environment. These connectors are like gateways — you have to be aware of what comes in and what goes out. When stress levels become unhealthy, it's worth checking how you are connecting with others and the environment around you. Otherwise, you might be risking a burn-out.

A burn-out basically means that you are giving out more energy than you are receiving, plus your energy stores might already be empty. Noticing the imbalances creates a space where you can decide more consciously how to deal with unhealthy relationships or toxic workplaces. You might not be able to change everything immediately, but self-awareness puts you back into the driver's seat, where you can decide what to do next.

Your renewed focus on the present moment also has the potential to increase your happiness — and, as a consequence, your energy levels.

Mindfulness is now a very well researched practice, but, in fact, it is a very broad collection of practices that all work slightly differently. It is also a life-long practice during which you will discover many different benefits. You can start out very simply. For example, in a leadership program I co-facilitated, participants were taught simple techniques such as focusing on their breath. Afterwards, they reported that remembering to breathe increased their ability to think clearly in stressful situations. Mindfulness does not always have to be a seated meditation. There are many levels of mindfulness, from just taking a couple of deep, relaxing breaths while walking to meditating deeply and sitting still for hours.

From my experience, mindfulness has seven foundational practices. A simplified description of what to do is: pause, relax, observe, discover. The seven practices all work along these lines and have different areas on which you focus. In an ideal world, you would eventually learn to practise all of them.

Explore what works for you and your current situation. Think about ways of integrating the seven foundational practices into your daily routines:

1. Mindful of body
Use your five senses to observe and notice any physical sensations, such as tension, warmth, cold, tingling, pain. How many different levels of detail can you sense?

2. Mindful of feelings

Notice how you react to a stimulus. Do you feel it is pleasant, neutral or unpleasant? How would you label the accompanying emotion?

3. Mindful of thoughts

Notice that you are not your thoughts. Is what you are thinking supporting you or negatively impacting you?

4. Mindful of mindset

Notice how you make meaning. What beliefs, values, life experiences define your deeply held views? Do you operate from an empowered state of being or a victim mindset?

5. Mindful of movement and balance

Become aware of what your place in the world is in this moment. Where are you in relation to other things, places, beings? How do you move through the world?

6. Aware of context environments

Notice how things and beings around you manifest at this moment. Based on the law of nature, everything is always in flux and changing. Nothing is ever static.

7. Aware of energy flows

Notice how everything is always connected. Some ancient wisdom traditions call this 'life force' or 'chi'. Indigenous cultures see all beings as family and are guided by this concept of oneness. For you as leader, it is important to notice what gives you energy and what drains you of energy.

These seven areas are called practices because you have to do them and do them on a regular basis. Just knowing about them doesn't give you the benefits. Most of the practices are pretty simple, however, they are not easy. But just starting with a few will provide you with plenty of benefits.

If you are just starting out, apps like CALM or Headspace give you a very solid introduction and you will only need ten minutes per day. Or you may like to jump right in and learn one of the original meditation techniques that has been around for more than 2,500 years — a ten-day silent meditation retreat called Vipassana or insight meditation. It is very challenging, but immensely powerful and beneficial.

2. Journaling: Discovering new insights

There are other ways of increasing your self-awareness by investing time in self-reflection and insight. Activities like journaling give you some insight into your thoughts and emotions. Writing them down can be a clarifying and hugely beneficial process. However, it has its limits, as you often automatically focus on either the past or the future from an intellectual perspective. It requires extra effort to gain insight into the present moment and trust your physical and spiritual intelligence more than your thinking mind. Thus, journaling is better used as a complementary process.

Whichever way you choose, you will discover something new about yourself and your environments. The whole process is like peeling an onion — there is always another layer. Capturing these insights in a journal will speed up your learning process.

Journaling can be as simple as answering the following five questions every day for five minutes:

1. What does my body tell me today?
2. What is surprising me in my environment today?
3. What is going well today?
4. What would I do differently the next time?
5. What am I grateful for today?

These questions are not set in stone. Create your own and make them work for you.

Journaling can help you to make sense of what you are noticing — either when you do your mindfulness practice or with any other situation that has come up throughout the day. You are reflecting on your self-talk and making the unconscious conscious. This is important, as your thinking determines how you act and this, in turn, influences your results. It can be an important realisation to understand what makes certain events so stressful for you. Everyone experiences stress differently and, thus, it can be an important warning sign.

This will help to define where you need to do more self-care or change your mind and learn something new.

3. Feedback: Considering external views

Asking for and/or receiving feedback from other people can increase your self-awareness. But it comes with a caveat. The person who offers you their perspective on how you show up shares and judges from their own, personal perspective. This might or might not be useful for you. Nevertheless, it is important to consider this external view and then reflect on how it might be a good springboard for a new insight or idea.

You might have already noticed that feedback directed to you often says more about the feedback giver than what changes would be really important for you. Listening carefully to other people's feedback becomes very important when we come to Chapter 4, where we will explore how to communicate more effectively with stakeholders.

4. Energy Map: Visualising your current state

One way of capturing all your insights in a holistic way is creating an Energy Map, a self-evaluation tool similar to the quite well-known 'wheel of life' exercise. The Energy Map is a snapshot of how happy you are with your energy levels in each area of your life. It gives you a quick overview of how balanced your life is and where to focus your efforts for change. A blank example and a completed example are both shown in the graphs below. You can download a template at www.ingridmessner.com/naturallysuccessful.

ENERGY MAP

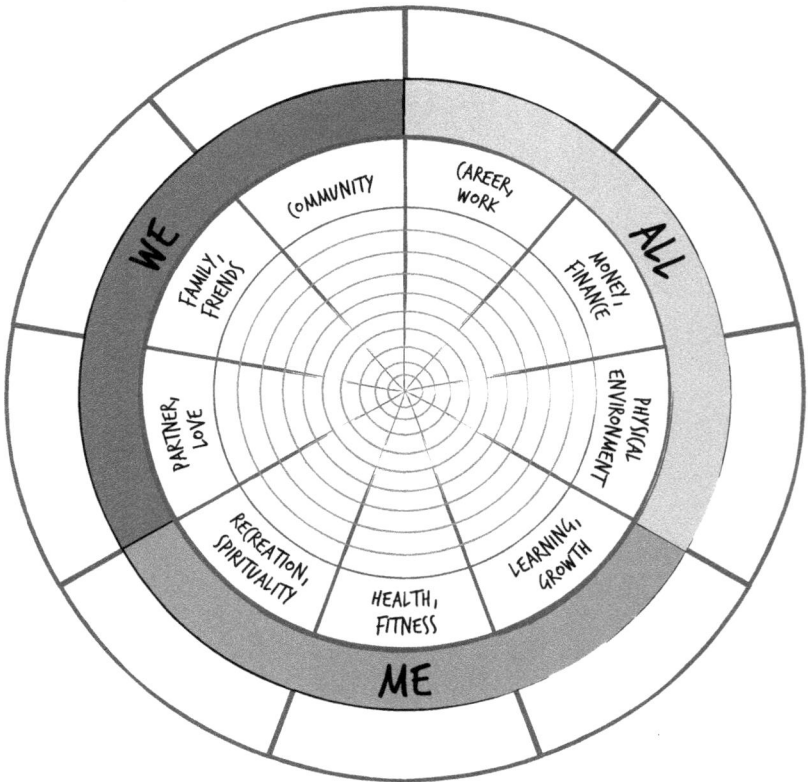

ENERGY MAP
((OMPLETED EXAMPLE)

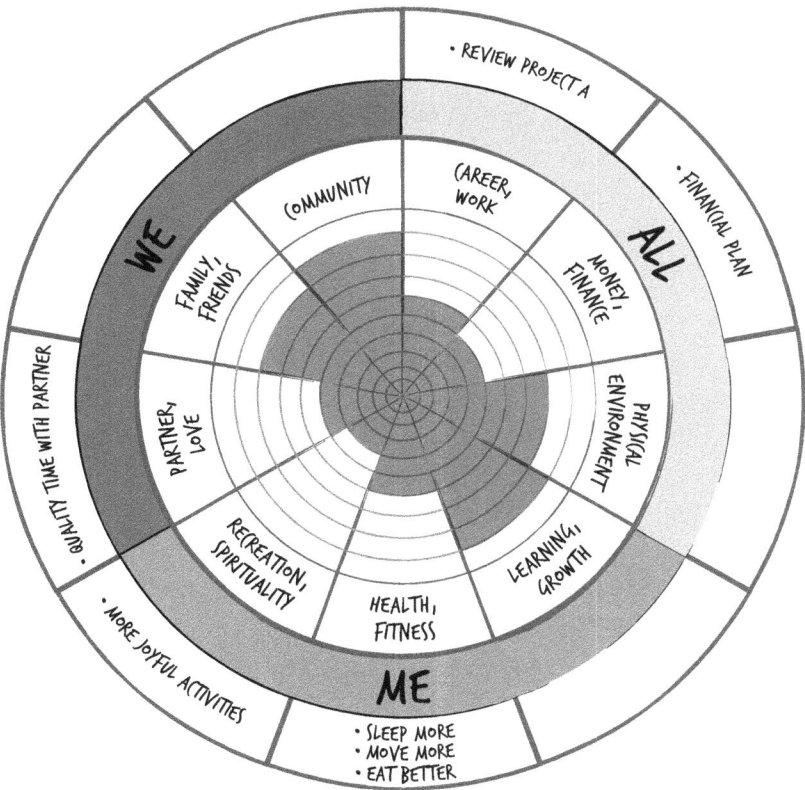

The Energy Map includes three perspectives of your life:

1. ME (how you manage yourself)
2. WE (how you manage connections with other people)
3. ALL (how you manage connections with different systems and environments)

Each perspective is made up of three segments, creating nine segments in total. These nine segments represent different aspects of your life. If the labels of a segment do not fit your current situation, feel free to change the wording.

Each segment has a scale from 1-10, where you can capture how energised and happy you feel in this area of your life by colouring in the circles. At the centre of the wheel is 1, which means 'I am not getting a lot of energy from this area at the moment and I'm deeply unhappy with this part of my life.' The outer ring represents 10, which means 'I am 100 per cent energised and happy in this area.'

In an ideal case, all segments would be at 10 and the wheel could run smoothly. If two or three segments are close to 1, you are facing a very bumpy ride with your wheel. Your energy balance is out of alignment. You might still be able to go on for a while, but eventually you will run out of energy or mojo.

It might be useful to remember that low energy levels often feel very heavy and dark, whereas higher energy levels feel more light, bright and radiant. These different types of vibrations are what other people unconsciously react to.

Start filling in all the segments to get an overview. You can then come back and add a few words to each segment that represent an important topic in that area where you would like to make changes. Do not think too long about this. Just remember any important insights that might have come up during your mindfulness or journaling activities. Writing this down will pretty quickly make it obvious what you have to work on to increase your energy levels.

What does all of this leave you with?

MORE CLARITY AND CONFIDENCE TO ACT

Increasing your self-awareness is an empowering process. It puts you back into the driver seat of your life. Instead of being run by your unconscious routines and habits, you have more space to wisely and confidently choose what you value and what you want to change.

Self-awareness puts you on the right
path to improving your overall wellbeing
and moves you from a stressed
state to feeling more energised.

Once you make energy management as important as (if not more important than) time management, other people will unconsciously pick up on this and respond accordingly. It could be your secret influencing tool.

When practising mindfulness, journaling and/or reflecting on feed-back and capturing an overview of your insights in an Energy Map, you will definitely notice how much more you focus on the pres-ent moment. The present moment is your only point of influence. Not the past, not the future. 'Be here now' could be your mantra in moments when it's really important to know what is going on — on all levels. The more you notice and understand, the more clarity (and less overwhelm) you will have, helping you decide more wisely what to work on and what needs care and commitment.

Once you understand yourself better, you will
also see other people in a different light.

THE ESSENCE

-SELF-AWARENESS-

➤ Self-awareness is an awareness of your internal world (body, mind, emotions, spirit) and how you connect to the outside worlds of other people and environments.

➤ Higher levels of self-awareness make the unconscious conscious and give you more control over what will manifest in your life. It gets you off autopilot.

➤ One way to increase your self-awareness is practising mindfulness, discovering more insights from journaling and feedback, and capturing a holistic view of your situation, including your energy levels, in an Energy Map.

➤ Self-awareness puts you on the right path to improving your wellbeing and overall effectiveness as a leader. It moves you from a stressed state to feeling more energised.

CHAPTER 2

ENERGY MANAGEMENT: PRIORITISE YOUR SELF-CARE

'The first wealth is health.'

RALPH WALDO EMERSON

	CONNECT	CARE	COMMIT
SELF	SELF AWARENESS	ENERGY MANAGEMENT	ACCOUNTABILTY
STAKEHOLDERS	COMMUNICATION	COLLABORATION	INFLUENCE
SYSTEMS	CONTEXT AWARENESS	STEWARDSHIP	IMPACT

On the evening of 13 September 2017, I went to my weekly hiking training session. At 7.30 pm, fourteen women gathered in the dark near the start of a bush track that leads into a national park near Middle Harbour in Sydney. Armed with headlamps and backpacks, we made our way deep into the steep, rocky bushland. We enjoyed our time in nature and met some amazing creatures like snakes and wallabies. It's quite tough physical exercise, but we also chatted along the way.

Two and a half hours later, on the way back, my left foot got stuck behind a rock and I fell on one of the narrow bush tracks and broke the weight-bearing bone of my left knee. I couldn't walk anymore, and the pain was pretty bad. We were a long way from the car park and, given the terrain, it was impossible for the other women to get me safely out of there. So we called 000. It took more than an hour for the paramedics to get to us. They looked at me and decided that because of the uneven terrain, they wouldn't be able to carry me out either. Six firefighters came a while later and strapped me onto a stretcher. I'm pretty sure they cursed me while they took turns pushing me around trees and over rock ledges. After a while they got tired and decided that it would be much easier to bring me down to the water than up the hill to a car park. So the water police came and ferried me to a harbour jetty a few suburbs away, where the paramedics picked me up again and delivered me to a nearby hospital.

This is where my steep learning curve on wellbeing and self-care started.

It turned out that I had broken my tibia plateau bone in several places and needed surgery. Which is all I was told. No one told me anything about the long recovery process. I had no clue what to expect or what was coming next, and I stumbled my way through rehab for the next year. There wasn't ONE person who helped me navigate the complexities of the health care system or explained to me how to support my healing in the ideal way. Nobody told me that healing requires lifestyle changes or that there is no magic bullet solution. This was very disappointing.

> *You have to make self-care your priority — no one else will do it for you.*

The general consensus is that after surgery, you do physiotherapy. That's it. Nothing else needed. No supplements, no dietary require-ments, no emotional support. It was frustrating and I didn't believe that my recovery could or should be so basic. I decided to run my own case and quickly became an expert on the different options for healing better, faster and in less expensive and time-consuming ways. I was very keen to get back to bushwalking again — as quickly as possible. I had to organise my own self-care program of healthy food, including functional medicine supplements, enough quality sleep, daily incremental movements, meditation, a positive mindset, a focus on my purpose, and supportive friends who got me through the emotional rollercoaster of frustrating rehab.

The point is that self-care is a systemic approach that is the foundation of sustainable wellbeing and performance. It takes a bit of trial and error before you find what works for you. It is never a fixed or linear process.

I tried and tested a lot and made an amazing recovery. Roughly a year after the accident, I started bushwalking again. My overall physical fitness is better than before and my patience and resilience have definitely grown, but that's only because I prioritised my own health and wellbeing — injury or not, you must do this too!

ENERGY OVER TIME

Our bodies have evolved slowly over thousands and thousands of years — in alignment with the natural environment. As leadership expert Richard Barrett puts it in his book *The New Leadership Paradigm*:

> *'Evolution would never have happened if all entities and group structure that exist today had not found a symbiotic way of living with each other and their physical environment, a way of living that minimised stress. You cannot exist as an entity or group structure in the physical world if you are not able to keep everything in balance.'*

Human beings are natural organism systems that have specific vital needs. These needs have not changed just because we have a faster, more virtually connected and technology-oriented lifestyle. These basic needs must still be met to support you to function and perform well. Ignoring or violating these laws of nature has negative impacts over time. Increasing stress levels and decreasing health and well-being are just some of the challenges that arise out of imbalances. Practising intentional self-care puts you back into alignment with the natural flow of life. It reduces negative stress, prevents burn-out and makes work and life more effortless.

Nowadays, we often talk about a shortage of time, when what we actually have is a shortage of well-balanced and aligned energies. Because we don't always understand this, we end up putting a lot of effort into the least effective performance-enhancing areas.

Energy management is more
important than time management.

Time is a finite, artificially defined resource. It is the only fair resource on Earth, as every person gets twenty-four hours per day. Energy, on the other hand, is an infinite and naturally occurring resource. If you practise balanced self-care and manage your energy levels well, you can have more energy per time unit and then use this to achieve more in less time.

The energy you bring to your work is often more important than what you say or do. Other people unconsciously react to how you show up as a leader. If you are not well, you will unconsciously radiate parts of your own struggles onto other people. These energy levels are contagious — unless you manage to consciously block them out.

Thus, the most kind and effective thing
that you can do for yourself and other
people is to show up as the best, most
energised version of yourself.

PUT YOUR PERFORMANCE FIRST

A few months ago, I was coaching the senior leaders of a global technology company. Their teams were spread across all time zones. Meetings could happen any time of the day or night. Many people in the program were only sleeping two or three hours a night — for extended periods. Performance suffered. They tried all sorts of improvement mechanisms before eventually realising that a lack of sleep was one of the main contributing factors to bad communication and decisions. When these leaders decided to make self-care a high priority again, performance improved very quickly.

The vibration of a calm and confident body and mind is different from that of a confused and chaotic one. Positivity is definitely contagious and very much needed to spread optimism, hope and joy in challenging times.

However, taking care of oneself often feels very indulgent. We believe that we are doing something only for us, not for others. Usually, when the outside world becomes more and more demanding and crazy, physical exercise, good food, enough sleep and meetings with friends are the first things to go. I am sure that you have experienced this. We all have.

This might be fine for a short time, but not for a long time. It is estimated that about twenty to thirty per cent of all fatal road accidents in Australia are caused by tiredness. On the road, the consequences of a tired brain not working properly are very obvious. The same is true for workplaces.

Fatigue kills performance. Thus, self-care is not selfish, but actually a service to the whole community.

So, ask yourself, what would an effective approach to self-care look like for you?

SELF-CARE IS YOUR SECRET ENERGISER

Self-care is the management of your personal energy balance. It includes all healthy and wholesome care activities that have the potential to improve your holistic wellbeing and performance in a sustainable way.

It needs a personalised, systemic approach. Not just exercising a bit more or eating a little bit healthier. Think about how you can enhance your physical, mental, emotional and/or spiritual wellbeing, plus the energy coming from your social connections and the different natural environments that you connect with. This includes all the areas that you have named as segments in your Energy Map (see page 32).

Self-care is not exactly a new leadership practice. In the 1980s, in his classic bestselling leadership book *7 Habits of Highly Successful People*, Stephen Covey listed continuous improvement and personal and professional renewal as habit number seven: 'Sharpen the Saw'. Covey defines 'sharpening the saw' as preserving and enhancing the greatest asset you have — you. He sees it as having a balanced program for self-renewal in four key areas of your life: physical, social/emotional, mental and spiritual.

Even before the 20th century, different ways of living based on ancient wisdom were proven to support wellbeing. Stephen Ilardi, associate professor of clinical psychology at the University of Kansas, came up with something called Caveman Therapy. He looked at our hunter-gatherer ancestors and what we can learn from them. Nicholas Kardaras, in his book *How Plato and Pythagoras Can Save Your Life*, explored Ancient Greek prescriptions for health and happiness.

Both came up with similar recommendations. In their simplest form, they can be summarised as:

1. Eat well
2. Sleep well
3. Move well
4. Get outdoors
5. Be social
6. Participate in meaningful tasks

Each of these activities represents an energetic connection to either yourself, other people or nature. The more connections you are missing, the less you are able to function in a healthy, fully human way. 'Illnesses' and their symptoms show up.

Usually, you will find these six basic recommendations in any well-designed workplace wellbeing program.

I would add a seventh one: Think well.

Thoughts are energy, too.

Holistic wellbeing can only be created if you keep your mindset, your thoughts and your 'inner critic' clear and energising. The way you think about an event or a situation determines how you act and behave. If your thoughts are negative or muddled, your actions will not lead you to feel well. When you expand your mindset over time, you will get away from fixation, control and overwhelm and begin to make increasingly wise decisions. These decisions support your wellbeing and the wellbeing of everyone and everything around you.

There is another reason why the way you think about yourself is very important for your wellbeing. Your self-image has its own power: You can't outperform your self-image. Your beliefs about who you are and how you show up in the world provide you with an unconscious setpoint that pulls you back when you venture too far out. It is a form of self-sabotage. Thus, knowing who you *believe* you are influences how you'll feel and what type of results you will be able to achieve.

As a leader, you play an important role in connecting and re-connecting people to these essentials of wellbeing. Without these, productivity and performance will suffer.

However, you have to put your own oxygen mask on first — before you support the people around you.

> *The old saying 'you can only give*
> *what you've got' is still true.*

You won't be able to run on an empty tank. Your task is now to define how best to fill your tank.

CREATE YOUR OWN SELF-CARE ROADMAP

Holistic wellbeing comes from managing your physical, mental, emotional, social and spiritual energy. To achieve a positive energy balance requires you to first become aware of what is giving you energy and what is drawing energy from you. In some ways, it works like a bank account. When you are in the negative and can't see any energy coming in soon, you will feel exhausted, run down and highly stressed. Not a good place to be.

One way to look at structuring your self-care plan is to go back to the Energy Map in which you visualised your current state. Have a look at the nine segments of your life where you might want to increase your energy levels. You can influence your physical, mental, emotional, social and spiritual energy with different activities in different segments. They are all interdependent. Look at the segment you would like to change and ask yourself: What type of energy is missing for you, or what type of energy would you like to have more of — physical, mental, emotional, social or spiritual?

Following are a few self-care activities to choose from or use as springboards for your own ideas.

Physical energy (body)

Your physical body is the foundation for your wellbeing and performance. It needs quality sleep, naps and rest, good food, movement and exercise to function in healthy ways. The way you breathe has a huge impact on your health. Find your own way of unplugging from technology. Limit the use of alcohol and other substances. As much as possible, live in non-toxic and safe environments. A regular medical check-up with your doctor might also be a good idea.

Mental energy (mind)

Looking after your mental health includes a variety of psychological care activities, like becoming aware of your thoughts and mindsets, actively dealing with negative mind chatter, practising mindfulness and meditation, journaling to free up your mind, and staying curious and challenging your brain to learn new things. Check in with yourself to determine whether the beliefs, values and deeply held views that were shaped by early life experiences are still serving you. If they are no longer useful, work on letting them go or redefining them. Nurturing social connections, being in nature and taking physical exercise also help to keep you mentally fit and happy.

Emotional energy (emotions, feelings)

Mindfully sense your emotions without judgement, process them and/or let them pass. Breathe deeply when it all becomes too much.

Learn to say no and create healthy boundaries. Laugh often. Do something you enjoy or love. Learn something new to help you build confidence. Practise self-compassion.

Social energy (connecting with other people)

Choose wisely whom you spend time with. Nurture and maintain strong personal relationships. Spend quality time with your most important friends and family members. Understand people's love languages. Be aware and intentional about the balance between giving and receiving (social reciprocity and or altruism). Get involved in a cause and join a group with common interests. Volunteer or be of service. Reach out when you need help.

Spiritual energy (connecting with different systems and environments)

Find your purpose and meaningful work. Connect to something bigger than yourself. Meditate, pray, have a contemplative practice — whatever works for you. Connect with others who share your philosophy. Spend time in nature and discover moments of awe. Wild nature always delivers. Learn more empowering ways to deal with money.

Overall energy management (practices for all areas)

Set boundaries to control what energies you allow to come in and go out. Decide how much external interference in your life you will accept. Practise appreciation and gratitude. Take 100 per cent responsibility for your life. Be aware of finding the right balance between activity and rest, engagement and withdrawal, closing off and opening up. Value your time on this planet — each and every moment.

*The most important principle for managing
your energy is 'less is more'.*

Keep it simple. Find a couple of overarching priorities that you want to work on. There are many different ways to practise self-care. What might work for you might not be the right thing for someone else. The important point is to make self-care a priority in your calendar and just get started. Taking time for self-care is not always easy, but doing something small each day, week or month is a good start.

Most of these care activities only become beneficial if you find a way to hold yourself accountable and do them on a regular basis. After you have given something a good try and find it doesn't work, you can always adapt your plan.

It is worth remembering that self-care is there to fulfil your vital needs as a human being. All of your needs will change over time — some will increase, some will decrease. Thus, your roadmap to optimal self-care will never be static. You will need regular check-ins with yourself to evaluate whether your current plan is still serving you.

*An important question to ask yourself is: How
would you like to feel after you have taken
good care of yourself?*

FEEL FULLY RECHARGED AND READY

Managing your own personal energy balance is at least as beneficial for you personally as it is a kind and wise thing to do for the communities of people you come in contact with.

Leaders who manage to show up as the best and most energised version of themselves are better influencers. They spread their positivity and energy to all people around them.

They can do this because they have found a way to shift away from a stressed state to a more energised version of themselves. They have found a greater capacity to manage stress and increase their resilience. It is rare that they face serious health challenges on an ongoing basis. And if they do, their understanding of wellbeing as a holistic system helps them to bounce back better.

With better self-care routines, you
will have more to give to your
causes in more effortless ways.

THE ESSENCE

-ENERGY MANAGEMENT-

➤ The management of your personal energy is self-care. It includes all healthy and wholesome care activities that have the potential to improve your holistic well-being and performance in a sustainable way.

➤ Self-care is not selfish. It is a very much needed leadership skill. It is essential for effective, sustainable and wise leadership.

➤ Energy management needs a personalised, systemic approach. Think about how you can enhance your physical, mental, emotional and/or spiritual wellbeing, plus any energy coming from your social connections.

➤ Human beings are natural organism systems that have specific needs. These needs must be met to support you to function well. Ignoring or violating these laws of nature has negative impacts over time. Practising self-care puts you back into alignment with the natural flow of life. It reduces negative stress, prevents burn-out and makes work and life more effortless.

CHAPTER 3

ACCOUNTABILITY: CREATE ENERGY FOR CHANGE

'Nature does not hurry yet everything is accomplished.'
LAO TZU

	CONNECT	CARE	COMMIT
SELF	SELF AWARENESS	ENERGY MANAGEMENT	**ACCOUNTABILTY**
STAKEHOLDERS	COMMUNICATION	COLLABORATION	INFLUENCE
SYSTEMS	CONTEXT AWARENESS	STEWARDSHIP	IMPACT

Three inexperienced bushwalkers were on a multi-day hike in a wild, inhospitable part of a national park. They had one day to reach their final destination before their food and water ran out.

It had been raining quite a bit since they began their hike. When they reached a water crossing, the normally small stream had swollen to a wide, fast-flowing river. How would they get across it? The three bushwalkers paused and discussed what to do. Their original plan of just walking through the river didn't seem possible.

While they were talking, one bushwalker got very impatient and pessimistic. He could not see any way of getting through the water at this location. He was very unhappy with how the river looked. He took his backpack and said that he was going to find an easier crossing by going back to a track they had passed a few hours before. There was no way of convincing him that there might be other solutions. Off he went — and eventually got lost.

The second bushwalker just wanted to get through the river as quickly as possible. He thought that 'mastering' the river would be their only option. He was optimistic and believed that it would all work out. So he took his backpack and started wading across the river. About halfway through, the underlying currents became so strong that they pulled him with them. He fell over and was washed downstream by the rapidly flowing water.

The third bushwalker knew that there was no way that he could rescue his friend alone in the dense bushland downstream — it was far too dangerous. They clearly needed help.

So, the third bushwalker sat down on a rock. He took a few deep breaths to quiet his mind. Then he started to observe the river. He noticed the different types of colours and ripples in the flowing water. He listened to the sounds the water made and searched for rocks in the stream. He sat quietly on his rock for a while, observing what was in front of him. Suddenly, he could see a way through the water. Carefully and slowly, he waded in a zigzag line through the water. It took a while, but he made it. He arrived safely and with all his gear on the other side of the river. He was safe.

He then set off and walked for another hour before managing to call for help to rescue his two friends. Help came, the other two bushwalkers were rescued, and all were well.

This type of scenario plays out everywhere and every day in similar ways, but in different settings. Exchange the word 'river' for 'project' and suddenly you are in the world of work. The story also contains some universal truths about achieving specific goals.

Pessimists are people who tend to go for the seemingly easier route and blame other people or circumstances for preventing them from being successful. They quickly want to do it their way and often avoid the real issues. They struggle to deliver results. The first bushwalker was a pessimist.

Optimists are often limited by goal-oriented tunnel vision that prevents them from achieving more with less effort. They often ignore the reality in front of them and think over-positively. They just want to get through and often get swept away in the process. The second bushwalker was an optimistic.

Realists, who are willing to patiently do the work, be agile and adapt to the twists and turns of life, are more often able to go with the flow and, eventually, reach their destination. They are more aware of the full situation — positives *and* negatives. They focus on each step along the way while keeping the end result in mind. They walk until they arrive. The third bushwalker was a realist.

> *When you get too attached to a tight timeframe and specific process, you often end up pushing the goal further away or burning yourself out. Delivering results requires very high effort or even becomes impossible.*

What type of approach have you taken so far to improve your personal energy levels and wellbeing? The pessimistic, easy way to a smaller goal? Powering on and optimistically thinking that it will be okay? Or accepting 100 per cent responsibility for fully implementing your own-self-care plan?

OWNING AND ACHIEVING GOALS IS ENERGISING

Your energy levels will not improve without your commitment and accountability. Your self-care plan will just stay a plan and not be beneficial to you in the long term.

Taking 100 per cent responsibility is what makes you successful and able to deliver on your accountability to achieve a specific outcome. Committing to and achieving new levels of wellbeing is energising in itself. Not just because your self-care plan is focused on how to build up your energy levels, but also because achieving any goal is satisfying and energising in itself.

Nothing breeds success like success. When you live life with integrity — meaning that you do what you say you are going to do — it gives you positive energy and allows you to stay in flow much more often.

Taking 100 per cent responsibility for your own wellbeing is a vital leadership skill.

The way you lead yourself is indicative of how you lead others. There are many parallels. You are not a fully effective leader when you are only accepting ninety per cent responsibility. What you are basically saying is that you are happy to give ten per cent of your power away.

In the framework of this book, your goal might be to fulfil all your energy needs and become so energised that all work and life become much more effortless. We all know from our life or work experience that real, sustainable performance improvement without accountability is not possible.

However, all humans face a struggle with accountability and have to learn to outgrow this unproductive pattern. Our nature is to look for excuses and blame someone else when things don't happen the way we had envisioned. The pain and shame of owning a mistake or not delivering an expected result is too much for many. Just watch a group of kids and you will observe this blame game happening quite a lot.

A higher level of maturity is needed to accept 100 per cent responsibility for your whole life and everything happening in it. Not every person will get to this level of growth. We all need to learn it, but not everyone is taught accountability at a young age. However, if you manage to learn from your mistakes and failures and take full responsibility for them, you can create new belief systems and feelings around specific mistakes you have made — and not make them again.

The famous basketball player Michael Jordan once said, 'I've missed more than 9,000 shots in my career. I've lost almost 300 games. Twenty-six times, I've been trusted to take the game-winning shot and missed. I've failed over and over and over again in my life. And that is why I succeed.'

> *Accountability is something that keeps you going — even when it gets tough.*

Failure and accountability belong together. Failure is not the opposite of success. It is part of success. And it is part of you feeling accountable for delivering a specific result.

Sometimes this can take a while and some deadlines might have to be moved when you learn something new. Overnight successes are a myth. They have been in the making for a long time. It is similar to the way bamboo grass grows: For about three and a half years, you see nothing above the soil and then, suddenly, in sixty to ninety days, it grows to full height.

In the end, it is down to you — and only you — when it comes to fulfilling your energy needs. No one else will do it for you. In this sense, accountability can be a huge opportunity for personal growth.

ACCOUNTABILITY IS YOUR
COMMITMENT TO SUCCESS

Accountability is the realisation that you are the only person who can make something work out well. No one else will take care of your self-care plan. You are taking the responsibility into your own hands. It is not like it is given to you. And this perspective of direction matters!

You claim the tasks of taking care of yourself. For example, you stop blaming a busy schedule where other people might have booked meetings for you.

You define clearly what you want to achieve and by when. You lead yourself and then get a team of supporters that make it easier for you to have the right knowledge. They keep you motivated by being your accountability buddies and checking in with you to see how you are going.

Accountability is feeling fully responsible for the end result.

Accountability is about delivering
on a specific commitment. It is your
responsibility to create an outcome, not
just work on a process or a set of tasks.

It is taking initiative with thoughtful, strategic follow-through. You do or organise whatever it takes to get the desired result.

It is important that you understand and live effective accountability for yourself before holding other people accountable for their integrity. Integrity means that you can answer for your actions and take responsibility for your mistakes.

Whenever you are unsure how you are showing up in the world

and how committed to success you really are, I recommend doing a quick check-in with a tool called the OARBED model.

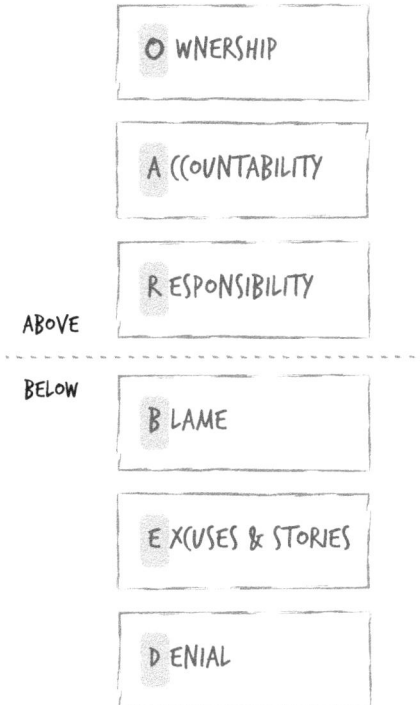

I often use this simple model in coaching. It helps clients to gain more clarity on how well their behaviours are working for them. They reflect for themselves on what they are doing and then place their behaviour on different lines in the model. The resulting clarity often triggers change and growth as a leader. Many leaders recognise their responsibilities and commit to full accountability, which makes them more effective leaders.

The OARBED model divides people's behaviours into above-the-line and below-the-line behaviours:

THE OAR-BED MODEL

O WNERSHIP

A CCOUNTABILITY

R ESPONSIBILITY

ABOVE

BELOW

B LAME

E XCUSES & STORIES

D ENIAL

Acting from above the line gets you positive results. You feel like you are in control and actively leading by choice. Above-the-line activities focus on what you can influence and do.

Below-the-line activities leave you in a disempowered state, always looking at other people and not acknowledging your own contribution to the situation. You are in the role of a victim — unconsciously or consciously. Nothing feels like it is in your control. You believe that either external circumstances or other people make you feel unwell and exhausted. It seems to be someone else's fault that you are not achieving your goals. Being below the line is slowly draining you of all your positive energy and life feels heavy and not very joyful.

It is important to realise that none of us is always above the line or below the line. Leaders float between the two. The key is to spend more time above the line and develop self-awareness for when you are below the line. Below the line, you are not taking responsibility or feeling accountable. You might be held back by some sort of fear, a limited self-image or a mindset that is not ideal.

Nevertheless, there is always one tiny action step you can take to step over the line, feel more energised and, therefore, deliver your desired results. Plus, by taking action, you will be more likely to achieve your goals. These action steps are different for every person and every situation. You will have to sense what might work for you. No one can tell you. Just go for anything that feels right in that moment. Action creates clarity and a long journey always starts with a small first step.

Once you have a good sense of how accountability works for you, it is easier for you to hold other people accountable as well. They might notice that you practise what you preach. You might even become an inspirational role model by being 100 per cent accountable for what you say you will do. Keeping your word builds trust. Trust means being responsible to another. Trust increases respect.

People will also notice how you deal with situations in which you are unable to deliver on a commitment or promise. Transparency in communication builds trust as well. You have to be able to explain what went wrong and how you want to improve on it. It is in the moments of admitting failure that growth and inspiration can happen.

All in all, accountability is one important way of making sure that a current situation is improved or important projects are finished.

So, what are the key elements for successful accountability?

PRACTISING ACCOUNTABILITY EFFECTIVELY

Before you even think about how to become better at holding yourself or other people accountable, it would be helpful to check in with your thoughts. Ultimately, your thinking determines how you judge a situation, and this determines your actions.

Your type of mindset determines how effortlessly you achieve accountability.

Review the list below and ask yourself which mindset you are in.

- **Fixed mindset**: You can only see one way of achieving your goals.

- **Acceptance mindset**: You are constantly fixated on achieving your goal. You accept whatever challenge comes your way and constantly change course.

- **Growth mindset**: You know that you can learn and improve, and you accept that, sometimes, you might not be there yet.

- **Integrated mindset**: You have realised that complexity, contradictions and change are normal constants of life. You use these as different perspectives and surrender to the flow of life while still being intentional about where you would like to get to. Failures are stepping stones on your way to successfully delivering a specific result.

Once you have finished your honest check-in to determine your current mindset, decide what additional perspective might help you to operate more often from an integrated mindset. This is the first task on your accountability to-do list.

There are seven success factors that make accountability effective:

1. Purpose
2. Expectations
3. Capability
4. Measurement
5. Feedback
6. Consequences
7. Communication

To improve your energy levels and decrease your stress, you need to focus on how best to fulfil your self-care practices. This means that you have to define what all seven success factors mean to you at this moment. Your definitions might change over time, but you need one clear plan on how to move to your next energy level.

You need to get more clarity on...

1. Purpose
Why do I want to do this?

If your why is strong enough, you'll figure out how to get it. Purpose gives you a more enduring motivation. To get to a specific outcome, some leaders are 100 per cent goal-oriented while others are more driven by their purpose. In most cases, it is a combination of the two motivations that gets them there. Thus, it is crucial to know your WHY.

2. Expectations
What do I want to achieve and by when?

Be very clear about your goals. Write them down. Your goals can be your guiding lights in dark moments. They can give you a sense of direction. By holding them lightly, you will still be able to take some detours if necessary — without stressing out about the most direct way to reach them. A sense of urgency derived from acknowledging the preciousness of one moment might influence (but not dictate!) your timing for milestones.

3. Capability
Do I know how to do this or will I need support?

Knowing you are capable of doing the task you have set yourself gives you confidence and trust that it will be possible. Even if you do not know yet how to do it, knowing how or where to get help will be a good starting point.

Support can mean that you or someone else has the skills, or you have a system that supports you. Ultimately, you want to create your own system of habits and routines so that you don't have to think about it anymore. You do it because you have decided once to do it this way. To successfully improve your self-care, you might need to form a few new habits. In his book *Atomic Habits*, author James Clear offers a clear process for how to do this. He also says, 'You do not rise to the level of your goals. You fall to the level of your systems.' Your system could be as simple as scheduling self-care in your calendar or having a buddy system with regular check-ins.

4. Measurement
How will I know that it works?

Tracking your results will give you awareness of the reality; reporting it to someone else makes you feel accountable and increases your rate of success. There is some value in reporting back to yourself, but it is too easy to cheat.

5. Feedback
How will I notice my progress and results, or do I need someone to give me feedback?

If you are holding someone else accountable, regular check-ins are absolutely mandatory. Be proactive with these.

6. Consequences
What will happen if I don't achieve my desired outcome?

Defining realistic and reasonable consequences is not always easy. In some instances, consequences are very clear and obvious. It is beneficial to talk about these at the start of a task or project so that every person involved is aware of the price to pay when results are not achieved. Exploring for yourself what a lack of self-care might cost you can be a real eye-opener for some.

7. Communication
With whom can I talk openly and honestly about my accountability challenge?

Find a community of like-minded people to support you. The company you keep determines the standards you follow. If others understand accountability in the same way you do, they can help you stay inspired and/or grow.

The same process can be applied when you want to hold someone else accountable. Communicate clearly and make sure to get alignment with the other person so that they see the application of these seven success factors in the same way you do. This is an important skill to remember when we come to the stakeholder and influencing part of this book.

COMMITMENT PAYS OFF

Accountability is a vital leadership skill — for leading yourself and for leading others. Knowing that you are accountable keeps you going until you have achieved what you committed to in the beginning.

Thus, accountability is your best shot at actually fulfilling all your energy needs. Without committing to delivering your self-care plan, you will never make it a priority to invest time and effort in it. You might make progress but — most likely — it will feel piecemeal, not a coherent, strategic approach.

Real satisfaction comes from having
delivered on one's commitments.

By expanding your mindset on how to do accountability, you will get away from fixation, control and overwhelm and turn towards wise decision making. Your stress levels decrease in the process. Your wellbeing improves. You move from feeling stressed to energised.

Your quest for effective accountability will help you to develop an integrated mindset, and notice and accept impermanence and contradictions in your own thoughts. It is about acknowledging and playing with the full variety and polarity of life. It can be uncertain and messy and yet very rewarding when you experience small improvements.

All in all, effective self-leadership, with self-awareness, self-care and accountability, is where insight leads to effectively applied wisdom. You become aware of specific wellbeing knowledge, practise and apply it, adapt it until it works for you, share it with others, and become an inspiration for others in your community. You can master your energy levels more easily.

Fully realising that it all starts with you and is also fully driven by you can be a huge energiser. People around you will want to have some of that as well. You have a lot to share, which will help you to create more influence and impact.

THE ESSENCE

-ACCOUNTABILITY-

➢ Your energy levels only get better when you are accountable for achieving a specific improvement. Accountability is about delivering on a commitment — one that you have made either to yourself or to someone else. The accountable You is not just focused on the process and individual tasks; you feel 100 per cent responsible for achieving a specific outcome. You do or organise whatever it takes to get the desired result.

➢ Accountability is one important way of finishing projects or improving a current situation. People who are not feeling like they own a desired outcome often use blame, excuses, stories or denial — trying to deflect their 100 per cent responsibility.

➢ To do accountability successfully, clarity of purpose, expectations, capability, measurements, feedback and consequences is needed. Great communication skills are a must-have.

➢ Your type of mindset determines how you handle accountability. The process of achieving the specific outcome is never linear and often full of failures. To deal successfully with this, you need an integrated mindset that easily accepts and adapts to complexity, contradictions and changes.

PART 1 – SELF

I invite you to take some time for reflection and explore new perspectives on **... leading your SELF.**

1. What drains your energy?

2. What gives you energy?

3. Which three daily habits would make a huge difference to your energy levels?

4. What is really, really important for you?

5. What are you committed to changing for your SELF?

PART 2

STAKEHOLDERS

*INFLUENCE AND
ACTIVATE THE BEST*

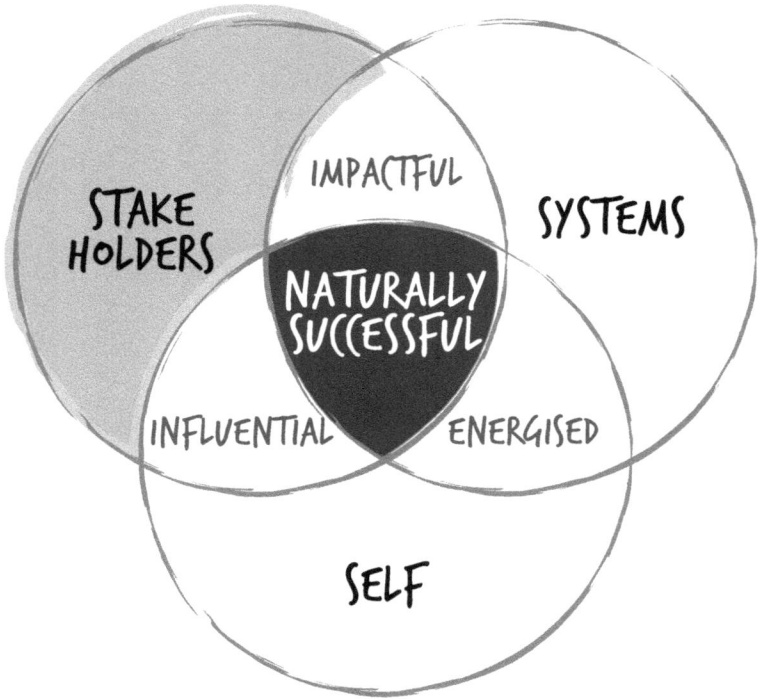

Once you have taken care of yourself, you are ready to take on the world outside of you: other people.

In most cases, you won't have the authority to tell others what to do. You lead without authority by influencing them to change their behaviours. This can often feel like a difficult and daunting task, as not everyone is on your side and working towards the same vision or goal.

It is good to remember that even though your STAKEHOLDERS have important roles and often fancy titles, they are first and foremost human beings. Deeply understanding how another person ticks, what motivates them and what will make them change their course of action only happens when you take the time to listen deeply and with the right intent.

It might take a bit more time. Communication and collaboration cannot be rushed and forced. However, investing in relationships usually pays off multiple times.

In the following three chapters, you can expect to learn how to:

- CONNECT more deeply with other people by improving your communication;

- CARE more for others by intensifying your collaboration; and

- COMMIT to your stakeholders by using your influence for win-win solutions, not manipulation.

Wise leaders bring out the best in others. You cannot create positive impact alone. It is a collaborative effort — even when it is 'difficult' and takes a bit longer. That's normal.

A Hawaiian proverb states: '*We* overrides *Me.*' Focus on community.

CHAPTER 4

COMMUNICATION: GET TO KNOW EACH OTHER

'Change happens by listening and then starting a dialogue with the people who are doing something you don't believe is right.'

JANE GOODALL

	CONNECT	CARE	COMMIT
SELF	SELF AWARENESS	ENERGY MANAGEMENT	ACCOUNTABILTY
STAKEHOLDERS	COMMUNICATION	COLLABORATION	INFLUENCE
SYSTEMS	CONTEXT AWARENESS	STEWARDSHIP	IMPACT

At the end of World War 2, my parents were displaced. They had to move from what is now Poland to a more western part of Germany. When I was growing up, my mother often shared with me the stories surrounding this traumatising experience. She missed her hometown and reconnected regularly with people from her former community. As a teenager, I often thought of this as being too sentimental. Life had moved on and she should evolve with it — no need to always revisit the past — or so I thought.

During my many travels and later, after I moved to Australia, where I spend quite a lot of time with different Indigenous people and groups, I changed my point of view.

I learned that in all Indigenous cultures around the world, it is a custom that you introduce yourself very broadly. People want to know where you come from, how the land looks in that area, what type of community and family you are part of, who your ancestors were and what elements of your culture might be important to understand. A first meeting with Indigenous people is very different from a first meeting in a more traditional business setting. Indigenous people invest a lot of time in relationship building, whereas in business most people talk about their roles and the tasks at hand or their earlier work-related successes.

Very often, you learn very little about the person behind the role before you start working together.

You're even less likely to learn about the country or culture or family they come from. In some instances, it even seems inappropriate to ask about or share this information.

Yet, think about a time when you've thought, 'If I had known this about the person I just spoke to, the conversation could have taken a different turn and had a different outcome.'

Let me give you an example. A while ago, I facilitated a leadership workshop for an organisation in the healthcare sector. The team was quite successful, but their culture blocked them from achieving even more success for their clients. They mostly thought of each other in terms of their roles and tasks in the organisation.

At the start of the workshop I invited them to sit in a circle, with no technology or tables to hide behind. I introduced the talking stick method to them — only the person who holds the talking stick is allowed to talk and everybody listens until that person has finished and puts the talking stick back in the middle of the circle. The first questions to answer were: 'Where did you grow up? Do you have any siblings? Share a childhood event that has been funny, interesting or meaningful for you.' These people had worked together for years … and yet there were many comments afterwards such as: 'I didn't know that about you,' or 'This is very similar to what happened to me.' In between, we all had a good laugh because the first person told us about the hospital they were born in and this started a theme that everybody followed. Hospitals were relevant in their work, so they immediately found common ground and had a sense of the area people had come from.

After this, the whole mood changed, and participants became a lot more curious about their colleagues. They noticed how important it is to know someone else at a deeper level before you start working with them.

> *Getting to know your stakeholders (or any other person) is the foundation for effectively working together.*

PEOPLE BEFORE TASKS

Effectively working together increases your chances of influencing another person.

In other words: Before you can influence another person to become active in a way that you believe is positive, both of you have to be aligned and on the same page. Alignment only happens once you become aware of what is there to be aligned. How well do both of you fit together? This is where getting to know each other becomes your vital starting point.

However, most people are so focused on the pressures of DOING that they rarely reflect or take time to focus on their way of BEING together.

People must come before the task
of getting something done.

Our way of being significantly influences the quality and efficiency of our doing. Doing is a function of being. Not the other way around. Whenever tasks are put before people, interactions quickly become transactional. Influence for positive impact clearly aims at more transformational results, and, thus, people connections have to come first.

DIFFERENT MINDSET; DIFFERENT RESULT

Have you ever caught yourself thinking, 'Oh my gosh, this person is really difficult'? 'Why can't they just accept my point here?' Labelling other people as 'being difficult' says more about your mindset and worldview than it does about the other person. The label is a way of blaming them for making your life difficult. You are giving your power away and not taking 100 per cent responsibility for your life and actions.

Ultimately, your frustration with 'difficult' people
limits your potential for influence.

If you invest more time in understanding someone's worldview and mindset, it becomes much easier to frame your message in a way that is relevant and meaningful for them, thus, removing the potential for friction and misunderstanding. You will find that you speak more of the same language.

Decisions and actions are driven by emotions, not just rational facts. Thus, understanding how someone ticks is invaluable for collaborating. You'll better understand why someone is acting in the way they are. This also helps to manage your expectations and prevent frustration. Frustrations with another person or a situation happen when reality does not meet your expectations, and there is a gap which you cannot see a way to close. You might fail to accept the current reality and start to suffer — unnecessarily.

For people to share their thoughts and emotions with you, they need trust and a safe environment. Psychological safety and a safe physical space where the conversation can happen are vital. Every person wants to feel safe, be heard and be respected. Leaders who create the conditions for this have greater influence and impact.

The more that sharing happens, the more trust and connection can be built.

CONVERSATIONS CREATE CONNECTIONS

Communication is about having conversations and interactions with your stakeholders that create authentic and meaningful connections. It allows you to get to know your stakeholders on a much deeper level. To become aware of whom you are dealing with.

Communication in this sense is a process of being curious and exploring who the other person really is.

For every stakeholder you come in contact with, you have to explore two different perspectives: the person and their role(s).

This is all about understanding the person's motivations and abilities on an intellectual, emotional, social, physical and spiritual level.

Their role or roles are determined by social, organisational and systemic aspects. Systemic influences can come from the industry, the market, regulatory or legal requirements, ecosystems, and community or society expectations.

The person

Understanding and applying the science of behaviour change is an important element for knowing how to best influence another person. Behaviours change when people have the motivation and capabilities to do things differently. Change is always triggered by specific stimuli, which are very different for each person. These triggers are complex, as they are formed over a long period. They are not always easy to understand, but can be powerful influencing tools once you have found them.

Your first step in becoming more influential is to become more aware of your stakeholders':

- **Motivations and purpose**: What is driving them?

- **Capabilities and abilities**: Knowledge and skills — what are their strengths and weaknesses; what is their communication and learning style?

- **Mindset and worldview**: How do they think and evaluate; what bias and preferences do they have?

- **Any potential triggers in their life**: How do they deal with feelings or emotions; what else has happened or is happening and important in their life?

Ideally, these conversations are enriching experiences for both sides that allow you to connect deeply and mindfully on many different levels and in a variety of areas.

It can be an exchange process, with respect, curiosity, exploration and discovery, that creates shared meaning on a personal level. Add the perspectives of the person's role to it and it will become a little bit more complex.

The role(s)

Learning as much as you can about a person's role will enable you to better understand what pressures and resistances they might be facing, and how that might be impacting your collaboration.

It can also explain what the social and system influences are that make them behave in certain ways.

Roles come with their own energetic charge, definitions and perspectives. They are mainly determined by the system that they belong to and cannot always be changed by the incumbent. Developing system awareness and understanding how systems work on an energetic level will help you to know the rules of the game and how to align with its flow.

Roles often also carry their own history, which can influence the person in the role without them noticing the full extent of this. They might not even know what happened with the person who filled the role before them, but some of the previous actions and results still linger.

For example, your stakeholder might be in a role that was traditionally part of the accounting team, whose leader had the reputation of being a micro-manager. This made previous incumbents quite passive in their approach. They all looked at energy-saving measurements as detailed cost-reduction calculations that they had to justify to their micro-managing boss. That is the current reputation of the role — focused on reducing costs. Imagine if the person currently in the role never questioned this approach — what are their chances for success when proposing a business case that requires a medium-term investment that increases costs? A specific type of mindset might be attached to the role — even when the person in the role is actually thinking very differently. You have to align your project proposal with the role AND the person — you have to build trust.

Trust is the foundation of high performance and great results: trust in yourself and trust in other people — in this case, your stakeholders.

Brene Brown describes in her book *Dare to Lead* the seven elements needed to create trust with the acronym B.R.A.V.I.N.G.:

- Boundaries
- Reliability
- Accountability
- Vault (you don't share anything that is not yours to share)
- Integrity
- Non-judgement
- Generosity

So, how do you communicate with your stakeholder to get to know them on a personal level, learn about their role and build trust at the same time?

COMMUNICATE MINDFULLY

It all starts with considering WHY you actually want to have this communication with your stakeholder. What do you want to achieve in the conversation (GOALS or higher INTENTIONS)?

When thinking about how you want to approach a specific interaction with a stakeholder, it is helpful to remember to not only plan for WHAT you want to explore or say (the CONTENT) but also prepare for HOW you want to show up or be in the meeting (PERSONAL BEING and DOING).

Some of this will happen in natural ways but, as with all behaviours, reflecting on these concepts can help you to become better and grow as a leader. I invite you to include all of the following elements in your preparation.

1. The WHY: Clarify your reasons, motivations and desired outcomes

Get absolutely clear about your intentions. What do you want?

- For yourself,
- For the other person,
- For your relationship, and
- For the cause you are working on.

When communicating to get to know each other, the usual goal-setting methods such as SMART goals (specific, measurable, achievable, realistic, time-based) are not very helpful, as most people get too attached to achieving them. And you cannot be efficient with people.

Thus, setting a rough intention will help you more to stay in flow and not get too attached to a specific outcome. An intention could be something like: 'I'm meeting person x to learn as much as I can from them about these three topics: topic 1, topic 2, topic 3. I'll approach the conversation with an open mind and listen more than I talk.' If you become too attached to a specific outcome, you might get a type of tunnel vision and miss valuable information that might pop up randomly during the interaction. An intention will allow you to follow a more natural flow and trust your intuition on what might be important to explore further.

2. The WHAT: Plan your content

To get more clarity and focus on the content of the interaction, I invite you to try the Integral Map tool. It provides a whole system view and opens up many different perspectives. Ken Wilber developed this model and I have adapted it to capture all the topics mentioned so far that are worthwhile exploring. The Integral Map can support you to see the forest, not just individual trees. It helps you to keep the big picture in mind.

You can use the Integral Map below as a type of checklist to evaluate which topics might be the most important for you to cover in your upcoming interaction with a stakeholder. Check what you already know about the other person and their role, where you might already have common ground, or where your points of view or experiences differ quite substantially. The map can help you outline where there are gaps and commonalities.

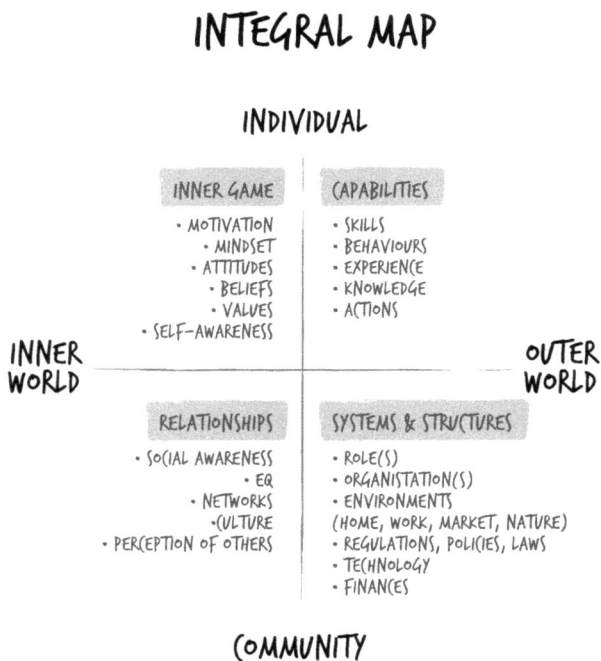

INTEGRAL MAP

INDIVIDUAL

INNER GAME
- MOTIVATION
- MINDSET
- ATTITUDES
- BELIEFS
- VALUES
- SELF-AWARENESS

CAPABILITIES
- SKILLS
- BEHAVIOURS
- EXPERIENCE
- KNOWLEDGE
- ACTIONS

INNER WORLD — **OUTER WORLD**

RELATIONSHIPS
- SOCIAL AWARENESS
- EQ
- NETWORKS
- CULTURE
- PERCEPTION OF OTHERS

SYSTEMS & STRUCTURES
- ROLE(S)
- ORGANISATION(S)
- ENVIRONMENTS (HOME, WORK, MARKET, NATURE)
- REGULATIONS, POLICIES, LAWS
- TECHNOLOGY
- FINANCES

COMMUNITY

3. The HOW: Think about how to BE and DO

Most of the time, it is even more important to be aware of HOW you want to show up in a conversation than WHAT you want to communicate. What energy do you bring to the interaction? Matt Church captures this beautifully in his book *Rise Up* with the statement: 'State is more important than script.'

So, what are the key elements of how to communicate mindfully to get to know each other?

The BEING

- **Curiosity and Compassion**
  Approach the stakeholder with an open mind and be non-judgemental. This type of mindset and attitude should always go together. You are here to learn something about your stakeholder. Assuming that you know them already does not help to build a good relationship. Empathy and compassion play a big role in this. Remember that everyone does the best they can in any given moment with the resources they have available. Sometimes their resources might not be fit for purpose. How can you support them to be more resourceful without forcing your views onto them?

- **Honesty and Authenticity**
  Be clear and honest about your intentions. Most people quickly sense if you have a hidden agenda. Even if they cannot voice it immediately, they will sense incoherence and automatically react to that.

- **Safety and Space**
  Create a safe environment where sharing openly is valued and trust can be built. Safety can come from a physical space and/or a psychological space. A safe physical space has boundaries

and a seating / standing / walking set-up that keeps shared information confidential. A safe psychological space can be actively created by you and allows someone else to express their emotions in a safe way, as well as keeping their mind working well. The way you show up creates the absence or minimisation of fear.

- **Presence**
Be present, in a real and authentic way. Multi-tasking is a myth. Neuroscientific research has demonstrated that only about three per cent of people can perform two challenging cognitive tasks at the same time. When you are in a meeting, there is one thing to remember: Be here now. Here and not somewhere else with your thoughts. Now and not in the past or future. Clear away any thoughts that prevent you from fully focusing on the person in front of you. Answering your phone is not always helpful.

- **Gratitude**
Develop a sense of thankfulness for the fact that another person is actually sharing something from their life and work with you. It is never a given or a must-do. It is a voluntary act. The best leaders I have encountered are the ones who recognise these interactions as gifts and acknowledge with humility and gratefulness that someone lets them into their personal space. They express their thanks. By doing this in a genuine way, they create a positive groundswell in the relationship.

The DOING

- **Pause**
Take an intentional micro-break before you enter any interaction with your stakeholder. Don't rush from one conversation to the next. If you do, you will always carry with you some of the thoughts and energy from the previous meeting. Becoming

aware of this transfer can help you to show up differently in your next meeting. A pause can be as short as a few deep breaths. Adam Fraser labels this pause a 'third space' — in between events. Managing this pause well improves your chances of successful communication.

- **Look**
  Observe and/or share by showing something or telling a story. When we are rushed, we often press people for answers to our quick questions. Slowing down and letting facts and knowledge emerge is more powerful in the framework of relationship building. Most Indigenous cultures value patiently waiting and observing in order to learn over simply asking questions. In most cases, stories create images in people's minds and stay with them longer than abstract facts and figures.

- **Listen**
  According to Oscar Trimboli in his book *Deep Listening*, listening is a skill that we are not taught very often and this is costing us dearly. There are many different ways of listening that Oscar Trimboli describes in his book. From my experience, one style has proven to be very helpful in terms of relationship building.

  A few years ago, I attended a weekend workshop to learn more about Dadirri — an Australian Indigenous people's way of describing deep listening. We learned from Tjanara Goreng Goreng, an Indigenous elder, that this ancient practice of listening goes far beyond what you can hear with your ears. It is an inner, quiet, still awareness that deeply connects you not only with other people, but also to the land and any other context around you. It is a bit like contemplation or meditation. The practice of Dadirri needs a lot of patience.

  You need to get comfortable with silence — something that not many people nowadays are used to and which, therefore, can feel awkward. However, silence might just be the moment when new insights emerge without you having to ask for them. Norwegian explorer Erling Kagge has written an international bestseller called *Silence: In the age of noise*. Silence has a lot of power waiting for us to unlock. Dadirri is one way of unlocking this potential.

- **Learn**
  Listening puts you in a space more open to receiving new information, whereas *telling* limits the exchange, as it often creates unnecessary boundaries before you even get started.

  A better way than telling (if you cannot observe) is asking questions. Be considerate with what type of question you use for which purpose. During the process of exploration, open questions are more powerful than closed yes/no questions. They will help you discover more insights. Closed questions can have an important role when you ask for feedback and or clarifications. They can sometimes speed up the process of understanding each other. As a caution, they can also be a distraction that guides you to a pre-determined outcome that might not be the best for you and/or your stakeholder.

  No matter which path you choose to discover new information about the other person, reflecting on what you have learned from them will be key to integrating your new insights and adding them to the foundation of a better relationship.

Overall, be strategic, deliberate and selective with your communication. Every word and every action carry a specific energy with them.

Telling usually leaves people in a passive state. If you want to create positive change, your communication has to be inspiring and positive. You want your stakeholders to feel empowered and take ownership. Negativity and fear do not breed effective, positive actions.

*Spreading hope and optimism
motivates more people to take actions
that will have a positive impact.*

KNOWING EACH OTHER MAKES INFLUENCE EASIER

You might feel like you have known about some of the above pro-cesses or elements forever. This might be true. However, based on my experience from coaching hundreds of leaders, it is very often the simple stuff that is not easily implemented and, thus, even though we all might agree on its usefulness, we tend to forget to apply it in a holistic way. Communication to build meaningful relationships with stakeholders doesn't just happen. It needs a strategic and con-sistent approach.

With ever-increasing time pressures and expectations from others, we can easily slip into the habit of putting tasks before people. We don't take the time to really get to know the other person as a holistic human being. We just press ahead with wanting to find a solution to the most urgent challenges. Quite often, this is when clients tell me about 'difficult' people.

*A quick check-in with yourself on
how you show up in these 'difficult'
conversations, and what you are actually
doing when you have them, might show
you that you are part of the problem.*

It is time to take 100 per cent responsibility for this. The good news is that, while you can't change other people, you can always change yourself. Thus, by showing up in a more present, authentic and mindful way, the whole energetic connection in a relationship can shift and you will achieve the desired results with less effort.

Having mindful communication and investing time to truly get to know your stakeholder might be challenging at first, but the better and stronger the relationships become, the more it will pay off when you start to collaborate and co-create together. In the end, knowing each other at a deeper level makes building trust a lot easier. Trust is the foundation for high performance in any teamwork. Without trust, you will have a constant battle to be right and to get stuff done your way. You will be left with a situation where separate individuals are doing their own thing instead of creating a community spirit where they are aligned and want to work together. Performance flows when people feel fully connected.

Mindful communication is one more step to move you from feeling frustrated and insignificant to empowered and influential.

THE ESSENCE

-COMMUNICATION-

➤ Communication is about creating meaningful connections with other people. Ideally, it is an exchange process with respect, curiosity, exploration, discovery and shared meaning. The intention is to get to know a person and their role(s).

➤ Labelling other people 'difficult' says more about your mindset and worldview than it does about the other person. Your frustration with 'difficult' people limits your potential to influence.

➤ Communicating to get to know each other can happen in many different ways: conversations, observations, shared experiences. Effective communication has elements of being mindful and present, having an open mind, not being judgemental, asking powerful questions, and listening more than telling.

➤ By getting to know each other better, stronger relationships are built. Meaningful and trusting connections are the foundation for effective collaboration and impactful co-creation. Mindful communication helps to move you from feeling frustrated and insignificant to empowered and influential.

CHAPTER 5

COLLABORATION: WORK TOGETHER

'When awakened by all things, the separateness of you and others drops away.'

(DOGEN ZENJI, GENJO KOAN)

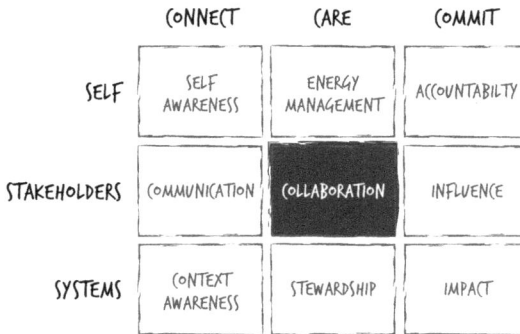

	CONNECT	CARE	COMMIT
SELF	SELF AWARENESS	ENERGY MANAGEMENT	ACCOUNTABILTY
STAKEHOLDERS	COMMUNICATION	**COLLABORATION**	INFLUENCE
SYSTEMS	CONTEXT AWARENESS	STEWARDSHIP	IMPACT

Susan is the Sustainability Lead in a large organisation. A few months ago, she discovered that a large project in her organisation had gone ahead — without anybody consulting her on its environmental impact. Because all project specifications had been approved, it was impossible to change any underlying parameter for the implementation phase. From Susan's point of view, the environmental certification outcome would be a disaster. There would have been potential for a much higher certification level if they had set up the project slightly differently. The company's reputation as a sustainability leader in its field was in danger of being tainted. Susan felt frustrated that she had not been included in the project right from the start. No one had thought of her and she felt quite insignificant and angry.

Luckily, her new boss asked her to develop a new and more ambitious five-year sustainability strategy. Her boss also encouraged her to invest more time in getting to know all relevant stakeholders. Susan met each of them individually — several times. She learned about their personalities, their ambitions, their KPIs and some of their current challenges. Over the course of a couple of months, new ideas for the five-year strategy emerged. The strategy drifted into areas that Susan had not deemed to be important before. Her internal network expanded, and relationships deepened. In the final weeks before the new strategy was to be presented and approved by the leadership team, collaboration with her stakeholders flowed quite well. When the day of the presentation came, she already had buy-in from all decision makers — and also from the leaders who would be implementing the strategy. Presenting the strategy felt to her like sharing the work of a whole community. The following discussion was quite short, and the strategy was approved with minimal changes. Susan shared this news with all stakeholders, and they celebrated the start of a new, exciting era.

When I worked with Susan, she discovered that the success factor behind the approval of the strategy was not so much that she had communicated more with more stakeholders. It was more about how she had approached them and how she had shown up in the conversations. She had focused on creating a sense of community and purpose, and nearly everybody had appreciated that. They felt like they were part of something bigger and more important. This helped to motivate them to support the strategy and its implementation.

The sense of being part of a tribe and doing it for the community is a powerful driver.

You realise that you cannot do it alone and, therefore, collaborate more willingly with others — even when you might not agree with everything the others do. You align your goals and work towards a shared purpose. Really caring about the outcome and feeling part of a community that is setting out to achieve something can be an energising and powerful experience.

DOING IT FOR THE COMMUNITY

I experienced this type of natural energy flow between people and their environment about ten years ago when I went to an Indigenous gathering in northern Australia. The Yolgnu women in Arnhem Land had invited our group to be part of one of their ceremonies.

In the early morning, before sunrise, we all went out into the bush and sat on the ground next to a cliff. It was very dark and once every-one had settled and was quiet, the women started singing. This song morphed into a sort of crying and loud sobbing. The sounds deeply touched my body and heart. Once the sun rose, they stopped. The birds started singing and everyone slowly walked back to their tent and campfire. The ceremony felt complete.

It was a powerful experience where everyone felt like one being, in some way like one body, and strongly connected to the land. The emotions associated with the crying just swept through everyone, clearing away blockages and opening up an empty space for some-thing new.

It took me a while to start to understand what had happened and what the purpose of this ceremony might be. We didn't get a lot of explanations before we attended. We only knew it would be a 'crying ceremony'. The experience partly spoke for itself, while some of my questions were answered over the next few days and some only years later.

From my perspective today, I would explain it this way: The crying ceremony is a type of community service. The women channel the grief and distress of the whole community and clear it away from the system to make space for new, positive emotions to arise.

In business language, you could describe this as a project that works towards a shared goal for the whole organisation. It is a community-oriented action. In Indigenous culture, there are many more layers and meanings associated with this activity. I do not know the details, and I would not be allowed to share them even if I did. The important point for me is that collaborating — like the women did — is an innate human need. It has been there forever. By being naturally successful today and caring to give it time and focus again, we help this powerful way of working together re-emerge. The tone and meaning of collaboration are totally changed when everyone is aligned and collaborating for a reason bigger than the individual self.

When was the last time you experienced collaboration that flowed easily and successfully delivered the outcomes you desired?

LIFE IS EASIER WITH ALLIES

In 2006, Jos de Blok and a small team of nurses founded Buutzorg Nederland, a healthcare organisation with a nurse-led model of holistic care that revolutionised community care in the Netherlands. They had realised that years of reforms designed to make their work more efficient had, in fact, compromised the passion and purpose that had brought them to the profession in the first place. All they wanted was to be able to look after people at home, and in a way that was aligned with their values and craft. They wanted a patient-centred approach, not a profit-oriented one.

Thus, they put collaboration at the centre of Buutzorg's model of care and operating model. They found new ways of working together in self-organising teams and put the patient back at the centre of their activities. The results are outstanding. Client satisfaction rates are the highest of any healthcare organisation in the Netherlands, staff commitment and contentment is very high, and impressive financial savings of around forty per cent to the Dutch Healthcare system were realised (as documented by Ernst & Young in 2012).

Buutzorg is an organisation with internal teams, and while your stakeholders might come from inside or outside your organisation, it will still be beneficial for you to think of your stakeholders as a big virtual team. In this way, collaborative teamwork, or working with one or several stakeholders, is an approach very similar to the Buutzorg philosophy and the potential benefits can have similar value.

Deep down, you know that collaborating with your stakeholders will get you better results. However, it often feels too time-consuming, too complicated and too difficult.

There is time pressure and you want the results now. You might also be searching for ways to get around certain 'difficult' stakeholders — just to avoid having to deal with them. You might even have tried to get to know them better — with mixed results. A collaborative approach has the potential to break down silos and connect you more deeply with other people. Communication can then flow more easily.

If you are not dealing properly with your stakeholders, they will be a constant energy drain for you and your work. Your relationship with them can become the elephant in the room. The issue is there, but no one wants to talk about it. It is blocking the success of your project. Collaboration builds trust and creates community spirit and morale. Improved morale supports a more supportive, flowing and energising work culture. When people feel like they are valued members of a strong community, they are more likely to be driven to deliver better results.

Increasingly complex and wicked business issues can only be solved by communities that collaborate, not by competing, ego-driven individuals. The old, hierarchical ways of working together don't work for most of the current challenges. Using the power of authority in your role often creates resistance in people when you tell them what to do.

One person alone will never have
all the knowledge and connections
needed to solve a bigger problem.

Collaboration helps you to solve these issues because other people bring different perspectives, knowledge and experience to your challenges. This is the same as nature's ecosystems. You are part of a greater whole and there is power in that. Your organisation and project thrive when they are connected to other diverse and complementary systems. You are part of a network of giving and receiving that is seeking homeostasis.

Great collaboration makes you feel more committed to delivering your promises on time. Thus, it often makes working together more efficient. You will be able to create positive impact because you and your stakeholders' shared performance delivers the desired results. Performance happens when everyone is fully engaged. Engagement is supported by alignment. Alignment can be created once you know each other well enough to properly understand each other's personalities and roles. Collaboration helps you to learn from other peoples' experiences. Thus, it can be a learning experience that helps you to further grow as an effective and wise leader.

So, what does leading and influencing others for effective collaboration look like for you?

CARING ABOUT ALL CONNECTIONS

Nearly all sustainability and social change issues are so big and complex that you need to work with other people to create some form of positive impact. Today, in business and in other organisations, your stakeholders often seem to be pretty clearly defined by the roles they have. However, collaboration can be seen in a much broader definition. To become naturally successful at collaboration, you need to go beyond tasks and people.

Collaboration is a synergetic, symbiotic and systemic relationship, where two or more entities work together to create something much greater than they could have come to on their own.

These relationships are also influenced by place, time and culture. The more you reduce the factors under consideration when starting a collaboration, the less likely it is that you will achieve satisfying and sustainable results.

To make collaboration successful, you need to consider three different leadership perspectives for the five core elements of collaboration (people, tasks, place, time, culture):

1. **Leading yourself**
   How do you show up in the interaction with the stakeholder(s)? What energy do you bring to the relationship?

2. **Leading others**
   How do you communicate with them? How much do you care about them as a person? How clearly can you express and align the overarching vision and/or goals? How do you create some form of community spirit and natural flow in the collaboration?

3. Leading in a system

How well are you aware of the spaces you collaborate in — the physical places, timeframes, cultural principles? How do you create the necessary spaces where other people and your relationships can flourish?

We often forget to include someone who has a deeper connection and knowledge of the place where the project results will play out. For example, if your task is to improve the sustainability of your supply chain or the type of materials that you use in your products, it will be difficult to do this with a team that is only based in one country and has never been to the other links in the supply chain. Managing all collaborators for this project is a challenging leadership task.

On a large scale, The Sustainable Food Lab organisation in the USA (www.sustainablefoodlab.org) is a great example of what is possible in terms of collaboration in a whole system. Since 2004, they have supported various supply chain initiatives and collaborations among food companies, NGOs, farmer organisations and research institutions. The diverse collaborations bring together different skills, expertise and connections to specific places, people and networks outside their own organisation.

Closer to home, in Australia, some farmers have learned and adapted their land management practices by collaborating with local Indigenous groups, who have taught them traditional Aboriginal fire practices. These practices are based on local knowledge and spiritual connection to the land. It's a different point of view compared to the way many farmers approach the land today. It is a collaboration that requires lots of openness, humility and trust. The collaboration is based on place-based knowledge and wisdom.

Projects can be run in a quick and results-oriented way or, alternatively, can allow a bit more time and include more, or different, people in order to achieve outcomes that are more likely to stand the test of time.

A few years ago, I met an individual who implemented a Reconciliation Action Plan (RAP) in an Australian business in just a few weeks. The plan presentation looked very professional. The collaboration efforts to get this plan agreed to included mainly internal stakeholders. Interestingly, no Indigenous people were involved in designing the first draft. The whole project felt like a great start, but also a bit lacking in substance.

A few months later, I met someone from another business who had already been working on their Reconciliation Action Plan for several months. They included different Indigenous organisations right from the start, listening to them directly about what would be useful. It took a few more months before the project team felt that the time and people were right to finalise the RAP, but it was successfully launched with a cultural event.

The two ways of collaborating were very different and so were the resulting plans. I am not saying that one plan was better than the other, as they both had their merits. From my point of view, it is more important to be clear at the beginning of a potential collaboration about how you would like to run it. What do you want to focus on — process, people, results, influences on the bigger system, or other benchmark criteria?

Some collaborations need time to evolve and the right people to be there at the right place at the right moment. Many Indigenous cultures had their own ways of waiting for these ideal settings. They simply would not start with a ceremony if one element was not right. I believe we have lost a bit of this mindset in business today and, thus, collaborations that are rushed often do not deliver the best results.

A wise leader will sense these right moments
and influence others to join in the best way.

So, HOW would you collaborate for positive impact?

SHOW YOU CARE FOR THE WHOLE

Some projects look quite simple, and you might jump in thinking, 'I only need this quick input from my stakeholder. It should be easy to get their views or data quickly.' But it turns out that they might not be interested in collaborating and do not contribute what you were expecting. The project gets dragged along and becomes an energy drain and distraction for you. It is hard to make any progress and, after a while, you might start to get frustrated.

I have heard these types of issues often in my coaching sessions. After a bit of reflection and further probing, most leaders realise that they were 100 per cent focused on the task and forgot to properly include relationship building and pay attention to the process of how they were connecting with the other person — for example, communication channels, timing and other external impacts.

The success of any type of collaboration depends on HOW you work together. You can approach it in a very rational, factual way or add an extra focus on relationships and connections to the larger system.

When you bring the attitude of care to all your interactions, you naturally collaborate with more appreciation, alignment and aspiration.

Appreciation means showing you care about people and places; alignment is making your interactions creative and constructive; aspiration includes sharing positive perspectives and hope for achieving something great together.

With this attitude of care, you create a very different working atmosphere and your stakeholders respond to you differently.

Show that you care in every interaction — care about the other person, care about your relationship, care about the cause (environment, social, other SDG).

If you do not care about the other person, your relationship or the results, ask yourself whether this collaboration is actually useful or whether the task can be achieved in other ways. Starting a collaboration without the attitude of care is a potential energy drain. This situation would require you to be aware of your mindset to set healthy boundaries and handle the challenges that might arise.

Collaborating with care has three elements to it:

1. Appreciation
2. Alignment
3. Aspiration

Let's look at each in detail.

1. Appreciation

Appreciation starts with respect

People notice whether you respect them as a person or just respect their role. People who feel fully respected — no matter what role they have in the organisation — perform better. They will value your relationship more and, thus, be easier to collaborate with.

Respect grows from the inside out; roles are labels given to describe the external view. Respect is acknowledging the core of a being — good and bad — without judging.

Accept that no one is perfect

Accepting the fact that 'everyone does the best they can with the resources they have at that time' can help you to approach challenging situations with curiosity, empathy and compassion. Better understanding your collaborator's personality and capabilities will help you to explore what else is needed to make progress. You lead (and influence) better by taking ownership of the issue instead of blaming the other person for their apparent shortcomings.

Be aware of how much you contribute

Deeper connections are built on an ever-changing balance of giving and receiving. It is called the law of reciprocity. You feel like you are in service to another person when you bring enough awareness to the act of giving. You feel gratitude when you bring awareness to the act of receiving. Awareness, giving and receiving create a natural flow of energy in a relationship. Your role as a leader is to manage a healthy balance that serves all people involved. Setting boundaries can be a sign of appreciation.

Empower and nourish others in the right way

Relationships work best when you are aware of a person's different languages of appreciation. How do they want to experience the fact that other people really appreciate and value them?

Gary Chapman, who co-wrote the bestselling book *The 5 Languages of Appreciation in the Workplace*, defines these five languages of appreciation: words of affirmation, quality time, acts of service, tangible gifts, physical touch (a bit trickier in the workplace, but still relevant — could be high fives or hugs).

Effective appreciation and recognition must be tailored and delivered personally and must be relevant and valuable to the individual.

Pay attention to how and where people come together

Fully appreciate and play with the influence that certain places can have on people. Think of your meetings and communication in general. How do you set up the space and how do you move around in the physical collaboration space?

Appreciating boundaries and the energy flows between them can create the framework for more constructive dialogue. Think of an

Italian marketplace, for example. It is framed by houses and has a centre point and trees to meander around. People come and go, and they bring personal energy with them and also take it away. The place is alive and buzzing. Your space for collaboration can be like that.

Appreciation builds connection and trust
When people feel fully appreciated, they open up and become more motivated and productive. This positive undertone makes the process of alignment much easier.

2. Alignment

Alignment is about finding common ground first
This might be shared values, a common vision or a similar motivation and/or passion. Clearly outline mutual benefits: The well-known thought process of 'what's in it for me?' is universal. Most of your stakeholders will ask this of themselves — consciously or unconsciously.

At a minimum, you and your stakeholder should become aligned with a shared vision, common objectives and rough strategies, but not necessarily the detail of how to get there. This alignment at a higher level delivers clarity on direction and is more important than agreements on the detailed path that will get you there. There can be parallel activity streams towards a solution as well as interwoven actions. As long as everyone is moving in the same direction, it is okay.

Be creative by building on the positives of push-backs
Collaboration requires feedback and the project or task will go through many iterations before it is finished. Be curious and discover the positive seeds in negative criticism. A new perspective can help to adjust your course of action. By listening with an open mind, you can convert adversaries into allies by understanding and aligning

the interests of both. This attitude can help to make most conflicts constructive and prevents them from developing into showstoppers.

Make the connections and flows of energy visible

Effective collaboration is like a flowing river. There is little negative friction. Tensions can be used as creative springboards for something new. There are different ways of making the energy flows and connections between parts of a system visible and tangible for all parties. In its simplest form, using a few Post-it Notes to map out all the elements of a project is often enough to show the effectiveness and quality of connections between the parts. In a more complex situation, Organisational Constellation work can deliver new insights and results much faster than any logical analysis.

Sharing power is better than control

Attract, motivate and nudge to direct and control, and avoid *telling*. It is more effective to establish clear lines of responsibility and accountability so that everyone knows the space they can play in.

Add some friendly competition

Competition in a community / collaborative environment has to have an element of enjoyment in its process — it can't just be about the end result. Think of 'friendly banter' and fun, shared activities. As long as there is a high level of underlying trust with all participating stakeholders, competition can work well to stimulate better and faster results. Everyone uses the best version of themselves to create the best results for the greater good or shared purpose. Some agile work environments support this way of collaborating.

Be aware of finding the right timing for alignment activities

All events in nature (and at work) have an ideal timing. This is the moment when all necessary parameters fall into place. By becoming aware of how to balance urgency with patience, your chances of ideal alignment increase.

Patiently waiting for the right moment is often a communication enhancer. Checking in with your stakeholder and asking if now is the right time to talk is a tiny conversation starter, but often determines success or failure. People have to be in the right space to work with you. Time and place are core contributors to this.

3. Aspiration

Tell a story
Share your strong desire to achieve something positive or great together. A well-crafted, personal story that follows the 'hero's journey' approach has the potential to change attitudes, opinions and behaviours. Researcher Paul Zak uncovered how stories that are personal and emotionally compelling engage more of the brain and, thus, are better remembered than simply hearing a set of facts. He describes how stories shape our brains, move us to be more empathic and generous, and tie strangers together. This is exactly what you need for effective collaboration.

Share positive perspectives and hope
Research has shown that doomsday scenarios don't work to initiate buy-in and action. Hope inspires action: If you want your team or other stakeholders to action a challenge, share stories of hope and heroes. Feeling hopeless about a situation is cognitively associated with inaction. Instead of being defeatist, look for heroes who are leading the way. Share the inspiration coming from their actions. No matter how small it might be. As a leader, your task is to build a counterbalance that activates the best in people. Auckland professor of psychology Nikki Harre recommends aiming for three to six positive inputs for every negative input.

Connect with your stakeholder's internal drivers
To encourage the other person to discover their intrinsic motivation to support your project, you have to first take their perspective and fully and empathetically understand their point of view. Then give

them a few choices for how to collaborate. Finally, provide meaningful explanation by sharing relevant context information. It is about giving them freedom within a specific framework and being open and honest about this. The whole process can align both of your aspirations.

By bringing appreciation, alignment and aspirations as care factors to your collaboration with stakeholders, you set the tone for a very human way of working together that has been successful for thousands of years.

So, what is in it for you personally?

LESS FRICTION, MORE FLOW

With all the care that you demonstrate for your stakeholders and your cause, you create an atmosphere of possibility. The possibility that positive impact is achievable if all relevant people work together in a respectful and effective way.

Blockages, push-backs and resistances are normal occurrences at work and in life. How you use these depends on your mindset and attitude. You can see them as challenges caused by 'difficult' people — which means you give away your power as leader— or you can see them as springboards for new ideas, improvements and solutions. The latter enables you to collaborate more effectively. You will notice that there is less negative friction and more creative tension in your relationships, which ultimately leads you to feeling a lot more in flow. This reduces your levels of stress and effort. It is like a river easily flowing around the rocks while slowly carving out a new riverbed.

This change of perspective and mindset makes it easier for you to accept differences in how other people approach a challenge. Learning from them and searching for common ground on various levels allows an easier alignment in the collaboration. Alignment creates flow and a sense of community. Really caring about the outcome and feeling part of the community who is setting out to achieve this can be an energising and powerful experience. There is an energy flow that connects everyone on the project.

Fully realising that a focus on people is always more important than just dealing with the tasks at hand also allows you to add more awareness of place, time and culture as success-influencing elements. People's actions are influenced by these factors.

Taking this more systemic approach to collaboration increases your chances of becoming naturally successful and achieving your desired positive impact outcomes with less effort.

Allowing different types of actions to contribute to a shared vision or goal requires you to keep your ego in check, trust your collaborators and channel all of the project's energy towards the desired outcome. Leading to influence others needs a lot of letting go and being okay with not controlling the details. Fully accepting this will change how you show up as a leader in the collaboration. This is a more effective and wise way of leading.

Collaboration with care provides you with a platform to be more influential and increases your chances of delivering positive impact — together with your stakeholders.

THE ESSENCE

-COLLABORATION-

➢ Collaboration is about working together towards a shared vision or goal that is too big to be achieved by just one person. Ideally, collaboration creates community spirit and natural flow.

➢ The traditional, hierarchical way of telling does not work anymore. Positive impact only happens once you join forces with the relevant people. You can't do it alone. The idea of WE is more important than ME. When people feel like they are a valued member of a strong community, they are more likely to be driven to deliver better results.

➢ Collaborate with appreciation, alignment and aspiration. Appreciation means showing you care; alignment means making interactions creative and constructive; aspiration means sharing positive perspectives and hope. When collaborating, alignment of actions towards a shared vision is more important than agreement on the right path.

➢ Effective collaboration ensures that there is less friction and more flow. This reduces your levels of stress and effort. It provides you with a platform to be more influential and increases your chances of delivering positive impact — together with your stakeholders.

CHAPTER 6

INFLUENCE: COMMIT TO WIN FOR ALL

*'The teacher, if indeed wise, does not bid you
to enter the house of his wisdom, but leads
you to the threshold of your own mind.'*

(KAHLIL GIBRAN)

	CONNECT	CARE	COMMIT
SELF	SELF AWARENESS	ENERGY MANAGEMENT	ACCOUNTABILTY
STAKEHOLDERS	COMMUNICATION	COLLABORATION	**INFLUENCE**
SYSTEMS	CONTEXT AWARENESS	STEWARDSHIP	IMPACT

In 2015, Architect Stephen Choi was looking for a Green Building Project that would make sustainability more accessible to a larger number of everyday people. A project that would influence the sustainability perception and habits of the larger community. Until then, only a few people who were already highly committed to sustainability were aware of many highly rated green buildings. There had been very few ripple effects in areas beyond the buildings themselves.

Stephen approached Frasers Property Australia to explore whether the company would be interested in creating an ambitious sustainability project with him. The Frasers' leadership team settled on developing a shopping centre complex in the eastern suburbs of Melbourne, Australia. Burwood Brickworks Shopping Centre was born.

After many conversations, a lengthy feasibility study and an international design competition for the project, the retail centre complex property targeted the Living Building Challenge®, the built environment's most rigorous performance standard. Burwood Brickworks is now, most likely, the world's most sustainable shopping centre.

Creating the property turned out to be a huge opportunity to learn about sustainability for the whole team, the tenants, the community and also the local government. The sustainability impact reached far beyond the actual retail centre. For example, it was discovered that about fifty per cent of the centre's energy usage was generated from retail tenants' use of refrigeration. Grocery chain Woolworths was open to exploring energy savings; they changed their fridges, installed high-efficiency lighting, and revisited the supermarket's construction materials.

And not only in Burwood Brickworks — Woolworths started to trial the new insights in other stores in Australia. A flow-on effect was also felt in other supply-chain activities. Ice cream brand Ben & Jerry's trialled different packaging for their ice cream. A new bus stop offered better public transport options and more cycling was taken up by the community. The discovery of toxic ingredients in some building materials, like lead and arsenic in water taps, led to the start of a consultation process to improve the Building Code of Australia.

Stephen's leadership approach to influencing different stakeholders evolved organically. He didn't set out with a list of the 'right' stakeholders and what he wanted them to do, nor have a predefined journey he thought they should join him on. He approached the project with the view that every person presented an opportunity to co-create a better sustainability solution. He had many conversations in which he offered examples of potentially more sustainable solutions to tenants like supermarkets, sushi restaurants or coffee shops … and then listened to what was actually possible in their world. He realised that no person sets out to pollute or do other bad things to the planet. Most of the time, owners just didn't know how to improve the sustainability of their businesses. Thus, instead of telling them what to do and then having to battle their resistance, Stephen listened, allowed a space for owners to voice their concerns, considerations and ideas, encouraged them to find a better way, and then got out of their way and let them do what they do best.

Stephen's and the Frasers' team approach seems to have worked well. The project is commercially viable and is already a finalist in two categories of the Urban Developer Awards for Industry Excellence in 2020: 'Excellence in Sustainability' and 'Development of the Year Retail'.

Burwood Brickworks ticks many, many boxes when it comes to how to influence community-oriented action and excellence in sustainability and development.

In a world of constantly changing players and structures, you will never have the authority to lead because of a given role or position. Nevertheless, most projects and tasks are only achievable if several stakeholders pull in one direction. Great influencing is the art of taking the risk of not knowing and/or not being right but still inspiring progress. Too often, leaders approach stakeholder engagement with a fixed goal in mind and just expect stakeholders to join them on their journey, instead of going with the stakeholder on *their* journey. That's a totally different game.

Wise Leadership means to influence and work towards a win-win solution for all parties.

INFLUENCE IS CRITICAL FOR SUCCESS

In many organisations and industries, the old, hierarchical, command-and-control leadership does not work anymore. People often work in teams to master complex challenges. Independent experts come together to create new and improved solutions. For most sustainability or social change challenges, not one person has all the right answers. Solutions are found in evolving, sometimes agile processes.

You might be working in a system of networks full of stakeholders who have their own points of view, ideas and agendas. You connect with them up and down in your organisation and across other organisations — even across industries and countries. As you do not have the authority of an all-encompassing role or position that would allow you to direct their actions; you need to become an effective influencer to achieve your goals. Your influence on a group of stakeholders can help everyone to work together more effectively. Influence is Wise Leadership.

A wise and quiet way of influencing becomes
especially important in larger organisations
where internal politics play a big role.

It is often impossible to voice your opinions openly without fearing repercussions. This can easily lead to frustrations. Choosing an influencer approach can alleviate this.

Usually, people listen more to influential people. In a meeting, this can make all the difference between your voice being heard or not. It can determine whether you are part of the crucial decisions.

Influencing with an intention to co-create a solution can excite stakeholders to be part of this adventure. By exploring the edges of what might be possible in terms of positive impact, you can bring all relevant stakeholders together and develop something where 1+1 equals 3+. Most people appreciate this kind of influence. It makes work more productive, satisfying and effortless.

Effective influence will work around resistance. It is like water flowing around a rock. When your influence creates a sense of ownership in your stakeholder community, they will be much more engaged in the process and more open to adding their gifts to a whole new solution. With lower resistance, stress levels are reduced.

Imagine a situation where you can see that some additional activities would improve the overall environmental outcomes of a project. The relevant stakeholders are used to a certain way of doing this type of project, and changing this would mean additional effort on their part. This is a typical case where successful influence can lift the game by striving for better results. Finding the courage and persistence to do this even in adverse circumstances is needed.

Being seen and accepted as an influencer can make you more respected and appreciated. More people will seek you out, as they know you can make things happen. Your contribution is a specific power to change things.

You have to become an effective influencer to achieve your goals and vision.

LEADING WITHOUT AUTHORITY

Star Wars character QuiGonGin is a Jedi warrior with special powers. His special Jedi mind trick changes other people's thoughts. After he waves his hand in front of them, they start to believe what he wants them to think —without them noticing the manipulation. It's tempting to see this type of influence as an attractive leadership style, but that's not how to solve our most burning issues. In the end, you as the Jedi Master could be wrong. Not one person alone has the right answer today. We need to effectively collaborate to find better solutions. Influencing is part of that.

For many people, the word 'influence' is still synonymous with manipulation or persuasion, similar to the Jedi warrior's trick. This type of influence implies that the people being influenced don't have the free will to decide whether they want to join your quest or not. There is also an important difference in terms of which intention you have when you start influencing another person or group of people. As always, if your intention is clear and positive, your results will most likely benefit all parties. If you want to be the only winner, your negative intention will drive the type of relationship you create with your stakeholders. After a while, most people will notice and trust is lost.

Influence, as I define it, is leadership without authority.

A wise, influential leader makes things happen without persuasion or coercion. All while being fully committed to creating a win for all parties.

You want to influence with authenticity, not authority. Influence with authenticity builds relationships based on free will, whereas influence through authority can cause a lot of resentment, resistance and avoidance.

Once you show up as your authentic self and become really good at influencing, you can be a true influencer. While you won't be the type of influencer typical of social media, you will be partly influencing others by inspiration. You might be so well known and respected that stakeholders want to copy what you do and achieve. It might be that they notice that you practise what you preach and, for example, lead a highly sustainable lifestyle or achieve great success with well-known sustainability projects. Influence by inspiration can be a powerful driver for change, but you can't rely on it for your daily work.

In day-to-day work, alignment of thought with your stakeholders can be difficult. You might discover that you are actually facing a clash of worldviews or mindsets. You know that if you want to create change, you will have to influence your stakeholder to change their mind. Influence always starts from a defined perspective — you might have a point of view that your stakeholders don't share.

Thus, sharing more and more facts won't necessarily change the other person's thinking. In these situations, it is important to take a step back and fully explore what the other person's perspective actually is.

SLOWLY DOES IT

Influencing others only happens when you fully understand the psychology of how behaviour change works, are clear about your intentions, and are open to being influenced as well. Be flexible; influence is a two-way street. No one likes to be influenced by someone who never ever changes their stand.

If you fully commit to striving for a win for all, you will have to consider what a win for you, for your stakeholder, for your cause might be. Only by bringing these sometimes very different perspectives on success together will it be possible to get closer to the desired positive impact.

Committing to win for all also means being acutely aware of what is driving you. For most people in the sustainability and social change space, it is not just about the money. Yes, you want to be fairly rewarded financially, but often being acknowledged by your peers and seeing your cause making good progress gives leaders in this space more satisfaction than a higher salary. Passion and purpose often cover the financial difference.

Influencing change with your stakeholders can sometimes feel painfully slow — it takes time to achieve outstandingly positive outcomes. But every small stimulus along the way makes a difference — even though you might not see its impact or results immediately. Influencing change often starts with just one conversation. Companies like the natural cosmetics producer and retailer LUSH see themselves as a campaigning and activist company. They encourage their retail staff to have conversations around sustainability and social change. This influencing approach is defined by taking a stand, and being patient and persistent. Some of their campaigns have stirred up and changed their market.

Influencing change is a challenging task. You don't have to do it alone. Sustainability and social change peer communities are your best support system. Having conversations about what has worked before, and what has not, in terms of influencing strategies can help you to get through challenging and frustrating times.

Even when your intention is to create shared results that benefit all parties, sometimes it doesn't work. An important point about influencing is that you must recognise when it is better to stop wanting to influence a stakeholder. Some people cannot be influenced. If you keep trying for too long, you are draining your energy levels without achieving the desired changes. The wisdom is in knowing when to keep going and be persistent, and when to leave and try another pathway.

Think of influencing as channelling energy like a flow of water. You don't want to end up pushing water up a hill. There's always a valley next to a mountain. Try that route and go with the flow.

COMMIT TO WIN FOR ALL

Influencing, a.k.a. changing your stakeholder's action, means that you need to understand all the factors influencing their behaviours. In its simplest form, this can be expressed by the following formula:

Trigger + Motivation + Capability =
Change of behaviour

As indicated in Chapter 4, you first have to get to know the other person. People are more likely to be influenced by people they know well and trust.

Building on the communication and collaboration activities from Chapters 4 and 5, you might already have an idea about what is motivating your stakeholders and what they are capable of doing.

It might be worthwhile revisiting the Integral Map tool and reflecting on the simplified version shown in the diagram on next page. I have added one question per quadrant. Answering these from the perspective of your stakeholder will increase your understanding of how likely they are to change.

The starting point for change is always an internal or external trigger. The internal ones could be random thoughts, emotions or memories. The external triggers are often place- or time-based. For example, a date in the calendar reminds you of an earlier event, or visiting a certain location again is a reminder to change something. The actions of other people, or even a smell, can trigger a change in you as well.

Triggers cause different bodily sensations that are picked up by our five senses. Humans are meaning-making machines and, thus, each person interprets these bodily sensations in a unique way based on their unique understanding and experience of the world. Triggers are cues that tell the brain that there will be a reward. These rewards can be negative or positive. The expectation of a positive reward causes craving and the expectation of a negative reward causes aversion. We either want to move towards something or want to move away from it. This is an innate human trait.

Discovering what these triggers are for your stakeholders can help you to find the sweet spot for effective change conversations. However, interpreting triggers is often quite challenging and needs time and skills. Observing, listening and asking open questions can guide you. It is fair to say that the following key elements of behaviour change are a bit easier to determine.

INTEGRAL MAP (SIMPLIFIED)

INDIVIDUAL

INNER GAME
• MOTIVATION

WHAT'S IN IT FOR THEM?

CAPABILITIES
• SKILLS

CAN THEY DO IT?

INNER WORLD

OUTER WORLD

RELATIONSHIPS
• SOCIAL NORMS

WHAT GROUP DO THEY WANT TO BELONG TO?

SYSTEMS & STRUCTURES
• ENVIRONMENTS

ARE THEIR ENVIRONMENTS SUPPORTING THE CHANGE?

COMMUNITY

The key elements to consider when you want to influence your stakeholder's actions are: motivation, capabilities, social norms, systems and structures. All these elements can support or hinder the kind of change that you would like to experience.

1. Motivation

Key question: What is in it for them?

Action: Talk to their values and motivations. Connect your cause with their values and motivations. Create a shared cause that they can make their own cause. Trying to convince stakeholders on a purely factual level often causes more resistance than buy-in.

2. Capabilities

Key question: Do they have all the capabilities and skills required to do the desired action?

Action: Share some insights and learning opportunities. Where possible, offer a direct experience or, alternatively, a vicarious experience.

3. Social norms

Key question: What social group norms influence them?

Action: Engage other people to create social momentum, peer pressure or social support systems.

4. Systems and structures

Key question: Are all their environments (home, workplace, market, nature) supporting the desired change?

Action: Where needed and possible, initiate changes to the environment. Align reward systems to support the change.

By collaborating in an effective way, you might find a way to influence the other person without being manipulative. By sharing alternative ways of being and doing that touch your stakeholder emotionally, you might inspire some level of change. Just sharing facts does not change people. Often, this makes them resist even more. Most people sense when someone is trying to manipulate them. This type of interaction leaves a bad taste that might taint any future collaboration.

To achieve the best positive impact results, you need to inspire and influence every stakeholder to bring their best version of themselves to the collaboration process.

These are their strengths, knowledge, wisdom, good energy and connections. The quality of input determines the quality of your output.

PIECING THE JIGSAW TOGETHER

There are some additional factors to consider when planning to influence someone:

1. Risk and time horizons
Depending on who your stakeholder is, you might work with them on an individual, group or societal level. These different levels mean they are facing different levels of risk when implementing change. Their timeframe of relevant thinking differs from short term to long term. Being aware of this helps you to better understand what their sweet spots for change might be. Wherever possible, add the long-term perspective into every short-term activity. How does this contribute to the whole?

2. Organisational context
When you start to think about how to influence your stakeholders and the system to join you in your cause, be aware of

how important your role / position in your organisation is. If your organisation's strategy includes sustainability and social change at its core, it will be easier to make progress than if you are sitting on the sidelines. Your personal reputation and brand in the market is another influencing factor. Next comes your style of communicating, building relationships and influencing. The context from which you operate is a key success factor, but not the defining factor over time. If you find the resilience to show up — again and again— and find executive sponsors who can be more powerful influencers, you can speed up the change process. Your sponsor might do your presentation in forums where the audience would not necessarily listen to you. It is important to be aware of internal and external forces at the same time.

3. Milestone measurements

As solutions in a complex system are not always immediately visible, it is important to be clear about small successes on the path to the bigger goal — otherwise motivation might decrease. If you can't see success, you often get the sense that it's not happening — when, in fact, it is. People in your team might need to be reminded of little wins. You might have to think about how you will measure your success. Whatever you count will be the focus of other people's activities.

Bringing all of these elements and perspectives together can sometimes feel like completing a gigantic jigsaw puzzle. It is complex and it takes time. However, throughout the process of influencing, it is important not to lose sight of your original intention and the bigger vision of why you are investing time in this relationship with your stakeholder(s). Most likely, it is well worth all the effort.

MAKE POSITIVE IMPACT SPREAD FURTHER

Influencing up to now has been (and unfortunately often still is) a power game with lots of persuasion and coercion. As more and more people become aware of this and reject it, leading in this old, hierarchical way becomes increasingly likely to create unnecessary resistance and fail to yield sustainable change. It actually limits your chances of creating positive impact.

Without direct authority and the power of decision making, you need to lead with authenticity. By redefining influencing as co-creating a win for all, you can build on the strengths and expertise of many different, independent experts. With the ever-increasing speed and complexity of today's' world, most projects and tasks are only achievable if all relevant stakeholders pull in one direction.

Influencing can be a commitment to higher standards and to striving for more. Co-creation, then, is the commitment between you and your stakeholders to come up with a solution that is better than any of the ones that both of you can currently visualise.

If you want to change what your stakeholders do, you have to first understand why they are acting in a certain way. Step into their shoes. Every person always does the best they can with the resources they have available at that moment. Be curious and kind. Explore what is driving and triggering them. What are their motivations and capabilities? Which social norms are limiting them? Which systems and structures are they part of?

Effective influence will work around resistance. You don't have to fight resistance; that will only produce more blockages. Creating positive impact is always a journey and there are many pathways. What counts is the intention of influencing to create better results that represent a win for all involved.

Your new, inclusive style of influencing can bring all stakeholders together to create new and improved solutions. Influencing with authenticity and not authority helps you to build stakeholder relationships based on free will, respect and appreciation of each other's strengths and perspectives. You build trust and enable more high-performance teamwork. Your influence on a group of stake-holders can help everyone to work together more effectively. Your leadership style overall becomes more effective.

Effective influence reduces your stress, makes your life easier and betters your overall success rate.

In this way, influence is Wise Leadership.

THE ESSENCE

-INFLUENCE-

➢ Influence is leadership without authority. A wise, influential leader makes things happen without persuasion or coercion. All while being fully committed to creating a win for all parties.

➢ Command-and-control leadership no longer works when trying to get people to create more positive change while also feeling engaged and not stressed out. Trying to convince stakeholders on a purely factual level often causes more resistance than buy-in. In most cases, your role or position as leader does not come with the authority to direct others anyway. You have to become an effective influencer to achieve your goals and vision.

➢ Influencers understand the psychology of behaviour change. They motivate others to change their perspectives and empower them to join them on their quest to create more positive impact.

➢ Creative solutions based on a win-win philosophy are usually more sustainable than solutions that only benefit some of the parties involved. Influencing with the aim of finding the former will give you better medium- to long-term results with less overall effort.

PART 2 – STAKEHOLDERS

SEEDS FOR THOUGHTS

I invite you to take some time for reflection and explore new perspectives on ... **leading your STAKEHOLDERS.**

1. What helps you understand your stakeholders better?

2. What could be your ultimate win-win solution with a specific stakeholder?

3. Which three daily habits would make a huge difference in terms of connecting more deeply with others?

4. What is really, really important for you in relationships?

5. What are you committed to changing when influencing your stakeholders?

PART 3

SYSTEMS

LET CONTEXT BE YOUR GUIDE

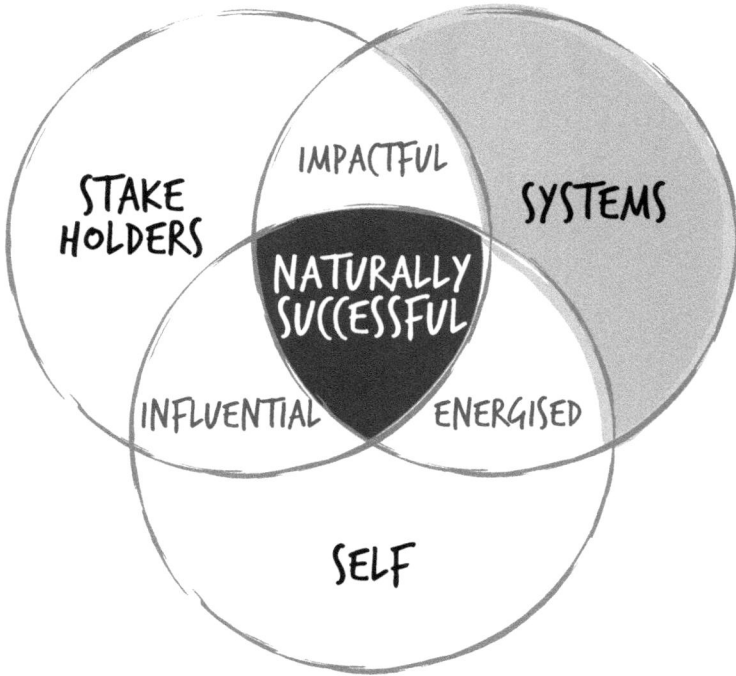

Everything is connected. You never lead or operate from an independent space. All of your work (and life) happens in a variety of SYSTEMS. You are always part of something else. You are interdependent.

All systems operate based on similar principles and rules. Not every leader is aware of these or fully understands them.

System awareness and seeing the whole affects the success of your leadership. Understanding context and important connections in a system supports you to find an effective focus on relevant details.

In the following three chapters, you can expect to learn how to:

- CONNECT more consciously with the systems around you by increasing your context-awareness;

- CARE more about and for relevant systems by defining your way of stewardship; and

- COMMIT to improving some systems by increasing your positive impact.

Change happens when you manage to tap into the right flow of energy and not swim against the currents.

Author Jocelyn Davis describes it perfectly: *'A leader's role is to channel the world's natural flow.'*

CHAPTER 7

CONTEXT-AWARENESS: SENSE THE WHOLE SYSTEM

*'A human being is part of a whole, called by us
the Universe, a part limited in time and space. He
experiences himself, his thoughts and feelings, as
something separated from the rest — a kind of
optical delusion of his consciousness ... our task must
be to free ourselves from this prison by widening
our circles of compassion to embrace all living
creatures and the whole of nature in its beauty.'*

(ALBERT EINSTEIN)

	CONNECT	CARE	COMMIT
SELF	SELF AWARENESS	ENERGY MANAGEMENT	ACCOUNTABILTY
STAKEHOLDERS	COMMUNICATION	COLLABORATION	INFLUENCE
SYSTEMS	**CONTEXT AWARENESS**	STEWARDSHIP	IMPACT

*A few years ago, I spent some time with Indigenous elder Uncle Max
Dulumunmun Harrison in the Australian bush. At one point, he
looked towards an area of dense bushland and asked our group:
'What do you see?' Everyone looked around, searching for something*

special. There wasn't anything extraordinary to see. He waited patiently and listened to the few suggestions that the group came up with. He then offered his wisdom: 'I see a big supermarket. There's food, water, medicine, fibre for clothes, wood for building, shade protection and many more applications.' Over the next few hours, he showed us some of the 'store items.'

This experience stuck with me. It taught me many things. The most important insight is one that Stephen R Covey also expressed in his book The 7 Habits of Highly Effective People:

'Each of us tends to think we see things as they are, that we are objective. But this is not the case. **We see the world, not as it is, but as we are — or, as we are conditioned to see it.** *When we open our mouths to describe what we see, we in effect describe ourselves, our perceptions, our paradigms.'*

In 2007, I participated in a workshop with Deepak Chopra, one of the world's most influential thinkers, teachers and businessmen. Deepak told us some interesting facts about how we sense our environment. To paraphrase what he shared with us:

Our senses create objects of perception. The world that different species see corresponds to their nervous system. Thus, there are many different worlds. Different animals, like bats or fish, see it very differently. Within the human species, the view of the world is influenced by culture, religion, history and other personal experiences. Thus, Western science is just an extension of our senses. Science shows one possibility of a human picture of the world. Nothing more.

How is this relevant for you?

Imagine your whole situation like an iceberg. Events, like day-to-day problems and challenges, are just the tip of the iceberg. Many leaders focus on what is happening above the waterline and ignore the underlying structures and currents that created the event. At the very bottom of the iceberg you will find your perspective and perception. These are sometimes called 'mental models' or 'mindset'. They are the basis for the whole iceberg. They determine what context you are able to notice and/or create. Context is the sum of all sorts of systems that you are part of. These systems determine specific patterns of behaviour over time, which ultimately lead to all events in your life.

This development process is never linear, but it helps to think of it like this:

mindset → system structures / context →
behaviour patterns → events

Thus, if you want to change an event, you will need to work on your awareness of the context. A small change in mindset and perspective can have a big impact on your results. It is like a ripple that shifts and changes the iceberg.

Let me explain this further by talking you through an example where leaders unknowingly had a view of the world that could have limited their staff's wellbeing and performance potential.

A client was just about to finalise a design brief for their new office space. Their objective was to improve the way their people work and create better wellbeing and performance in their team. They planned an activity-based workplace design. Before we met, they had not considered what the benefits of a more nature-oriented design could be.

Our bodies are connected to our environment: What we eat, the air we breathe, what we see, hear, taste, smell, feel … all these experiences have an influence on how we feel and how productive we can be. Humans have an inherent inclination to affiliate with nature.

This process is called biophilia, meaning: The love of connecting with nature.

Healthy people need healthy habitats and, thus, a healthy planet. A good work habitat is an ecologically sound and productive environment where people function to their optimal potential. Biophilic design looks at people as a biological organism in the built environment and creates these good habitats.

As we spend about ninety per cent of our time indoors, it is vital to design these workspaces in a healthy way — if you want to give every person the best chance of performing well. My client decided to add biophilic design elements to their new office space to create an ideal context for work.

Where do you currently limit your focus to the obvious issues popping up above the waterline? Why would it make sense for you to explore the underlying structures of systems and behaviour patterns?

INFLUENCE WHERE IT MATTERS MOST

You never operate or lead in an isolated or empty space. Performance and change do not happen in a vacuum. There are many influences you need to be aware of. However, too often, we tend to focus on the parts rather than seeing the whole, big, interconnected picture. We fail to see events, organisations, groups and environments as dynamic processes.

*A better appreciation of all these systems would
lead to more appropriate and effective actions.*

When challenges and stress arise, their cause is either inside of you or outside of you. The outside space is defined by people and a variety of systems. We have covered the self and other people in earlier chapters. Systems are often the missing part that leaders do not fully integrate into their exploration of data and decision making.

Even though fully understanding how a system operates and what elements are key parts of it is complex, any time spent on increasing your awareness is time and effort well invested that will pay off at a later stage of your project or task. You always only have to understand as much as is necessary to take the next step to run the next experiment. As everything is interconnected in the web of life, we will never be able to fully understand every detail of every system, but we can align ourselves as best as possible and allow ourselves to go with the flow.

*You can only influence and change what you
are aware of and what you understand.*

As a leader, you need to be aware of the conditions that enable the people you lead to thrive in a sustainable way. If you want to create positive impact towards a thriving, sustainable future, the first step must be to understand how nature sustains life. Otherwise, you are operating like a fish in water. You feel so much part of the system that you do not notice it anymore. The water quality could slowly or abruptly change, which would make you feel unwell, but you would not know why you were feeling this way. Consequently, you would not be able to enact change and would continue to suffer. Or, worse, blame the other fish for not feeling well.

Many leaders nowadays, even some of those working in sustainability, have lost most of the necessary system awareness and are no longer deeply connected to nature as a living system. We are facing a cultural challenge called 'Environmental Generational Amnesia'. From generation to generation, we forget what healthy environments look like and feel like, and how they function. Even if you as a leader in sustainability have a good sense of what a healthy ecosystem is, the chances are high that some of your stakeholders do not.

This means that, instead of only looking at obvious day-to-day issues and problems, you need to step out of the system, see the big picture, patiently dig deeper to understand all forces at work and then explore the best intervention points to leverage change. Sharing your findings by educating stakeholders is an important part of your leadership.

Working with the natural system, not against it,
is the foundation for your success.

The principles of nature are universal. Most leaders fail to integrate all environments and their context when making decisions in regard to the habitats they operate in. There is plenty of research demonstrating the positive impact of nature connection for humans.

Author Clemens G Arvay describes in his book *The Biophilia Effect* that something as simple as fascination with nature can switch your brain into a new mode. Humans have two forms of attention. The first one is directed attention. It is the focus you apply at work, when driving and studying, and for many everyday activities. It uses up our energy and can easily exhaust us. We have to actively maintain it and, thus, it can make us feel tired and stressed. This then leads to a dip in attention, which requires even more focus. It is a vicious circle that you need to manage well to keep performing.

The second form of attention automatically restores energy. It requires no exertion. It is called fascination. Researchers Rachel and Stephen Kaplan discovered that nature triggers this form of attention. Our brains adapted to processes in nature over thousands of years. It is familiar ground for our subconscious mind. The Kaplans researched 1,200 office workers divided into two groups — those who could see nature and green spaces through a window and those who couldn't. The ones who could see greenery reported having fewer problems concentrating or fewer frustrations with work than the group who could not see greenery. On average, they had significantly more fun working. The Kaplans concluded that nature is the best environment for restoring someone's directed attention through fascination and remedying the consequences of fatigue. Other scientists have come to similar conclusions.

By better understanding systems as context, you will feel less and less that you are working against a system that does not seem to support your desire for changes.

Systems will be less of a black box and more of a wondrous network of relationships, patterns and parts to be explored and tapped into. This reduces your frustration and stress, and the feeling of being overwhelmed and not knowing where to focus your efforts for maximum effect.

Context also determines the quality of your conversations with others.

Being and working in a different context and space has a direct impact on people, their performance and their relationships. As our work environments have changed quickly to more remote and online work — especially evident during the coronavirus pandemic of 2020 — people have suddenly begun to work in a very different space. Some might have more access to green spaces and some less.

When more work is conducted via video conferences, relationships with other humans become different energetically. It can be very tiring to constantly direct attention onto a screen if not counterbalanced by some restorative time in nature. Over time, people lose connection with the real world as they are glued to a much smaller circle of movement. The emotional and physical consequences of this lead to very different decision making.

*Higher levels of awareness make it easier to
be able to handle today's complex challenges,
change and chaos effectively and sustainably
with a positive impact for future generations.*

There are many different ways of explaining different levels of awareness. Sometimes, awareness is also called consciousness. I use the
two terms here interchangeably. The basic structure of these maps
of consciousness is that lower levels are more ego-focused and
leaders at higher levels think more holistically, strategically and
eco-systemically.

Most of our stress, overwhelm and frustration is caused by not being
fully connected to our natural, innate needs and not living and
working in healthy habitats. We are working against the universe's
natural flow of energy, which is like pushing water uphill — nearly
impossible and exhausting — and not sustainable.

Many of our organisations and leadership styles are still based on a
mechanistic world view, created by industrial production, machines
and technology. These structures often follow linear pathways and
see natural systems as no longer sufficient. Business has started
to use the term VUCA for the current situation. VUCA stands for:
volatile, uncertain, complex and ambiguous. This term originally
came from the military in the Western world and, thus, from a very
hierarchical, controlling point of view. Once you understand that
nature is a living system that follows different, more fluid and less
rigid principles, you realise that the term VUCA is expressing nothing
new or special. Nature has always been like this: volatile, meaning
always in motion and change; uncertain, meaning not controllable;
complex, meaning contextual; and ambiguous, meaning diverse.

The different levels of awareness (from ego- to eco-focus) represent
different nature mindsets, and your leadership actions are very
much dependent on how you understand nature. A deep nature

connection is crucial for your leadership to have a positive impact on people and planet. By deeply understanding limited natural planetary resources and ecosystems, you will make different decisions. This higher level of awareness and knowing will lead to increased positive impact on people and planet.

You protect only what you love, and you only love what you know well. You only know well what you have deeply and mindfully connected with, with all your senses — while being fully aware of your context.

It's like the difference between watching a swimming race on a screen or attending a live swimming event, or between swimming in an indoor pool and swimming in a rock pool or in the ocean itself. Your experience of what you see and how you feel afterwards is very different. You think about different things and see your environment in different ways.

So, what exactly is the awareness of a system in your context environment?

SYSTEMS ARE SPACES YOU OPERATE IN

During a trip to Japan, I noticed that hardly anybody was walking around the streets eating or holding a take-away cup or water bottle. I was mesmerised by the respect that Japanese people demonstrate for natural resources. A tea ceremony is a good example. You can just drink your tea in a take-away cup, or you can use the tea as a springboard to create a much richer experience that goes far beyond meeting your basic needs for hydrating your body.

A tea ceremony is an ideal space. It can create better relationships, offer a physical place for new ideas to arise, and introduce you to the world of a specific tea. You learn more about your host and can enjoy a pause for mindful, reflective moments. Plus, it truly honours and celebrates nature and human connection.

HOW this experience is created is highly relevant for business leaders.

Too often, we discuss performance and wellbeing without any reference to the context, meaning the spaces where they happen.

'Space' can be a variety of concepts as well as practical applications of these abstract ideas. A space can be a physical room (built or natural environments), the relational space between people, a way of collaborating, a cultural context, a state of being in a system, an interval or gap between activities. Basically, spaces are systems.

Well-known environmental scientist, educator and writer Donella H Meadows defines a system as: 'A set of elements or parts that is coherently organised and interconnected in a pattern or structure that produces a characteristic set of behaviours, often classified as its "function" or "purpose".'

Some of the system elements are visible and tangible, whereas others are invisible and intangible. Both forms affect wellbeing, performance and results. As a leader, you need to be aware of all of them. Coming back to the iceberg model as a reference point: Systems are the realities below the waterline that are often difficult to grasp, and yet they define all of our results. A big-picture view and systems thinking are necessary to effectively lead in a sustainable way.

The **tangible elements** are visible context environments, like:

- **Home base**: Understand the value of a supportive home environment.

- **Workplace**: Create a safe and inspiring workplace.

- **Ecosystems** and nature around you and your work: Consider all impacts of your leadership decisions and practise stewardship.

- **Country**: Political and legal systems can cause changes that will impact your work.

- **Planet**: Include global considerations, like the Sustainability Development Goals (SDGs) in your work. Population growth or decline is impacting individual performance. Freedom of choice is potentially reduced by a lack of space, safety and stillness. Competition around scarce resources reduces human traits like kindness and compassion.

The **intangible elements** are the relationships and energies flowing in between all the tangible elements and beyond. Many of these interconnections operate through the flow of information. These invisible energies create complex networks and communities. As mentioned in Chapter 3, being more mindful will help you notice more easily how everything is always connected and can influence you and other people. Some ancient wisdom traditions call this 'life force' or 'chi'. Indigenous cultures see all beings as family and are guided by this concept of oneness. We are all part of the web of life.

Over the past four decades, modern science has slowly been picking up on this ancient systemic view of life. Physicist and systems theorist Fritjof Capra, together with Pier Luigi Luisi, a professor of biochemistry, wrote a seminal book about this topic. In *The Systems View of Life*, they describe in detail how our perspectives and paradigms have evolved from the early systems thinkers who expressed the now well-known phrase, 'the whole is more than the sum of its parts'. This means that a living system — an organism, ecosystem or social system — is an integrated whole whose properties cannot be reduced to those of smaller parts. The 'systemic' properties are properties of the whole, which none of its parts have. So, systems thinking involves a shift of perspective from the parts to the whole, eventually settling on the now widely accepted view of 'Deep Ecology', which recognises the intrinsic value of all living beings and views humans as just one particular strand in the web of life.

Capra and Luisi state that: 'When this deep ecological perception becomes part of our daily awareness, a radically new system of ethics emerges. Such a deep ecological ethic is urgently needed today, especially in science, since most of what scientists do is not life-furthering and life-preserving but life-destroying.'

I believe the same is true for leadership in many organisations. It is also true for many individual leaders in regard to how they lead themselves and others.

For you as leader, it is important to notice what gives you energy and what drains you of energy, as well as noticing how you and your stakeholders are connected to all relevant systems in your context.

Once you understand these systemic space concepts fully, they will support you to create better results with less effort.

How can you do this?

MAKING YOUR SPACES UNDERSTANDABLE

Most of us are trained to look first and quickly at the most obvious and pressing issues caused by day-to-day events. By analysing facts, tasks, other 'objective' problem definitions, and sometimes also considering people and relationship issues, we scratch the surface and come up with a short-term, limited-focus and often unsustainable solution. However, as indicated before, this thinking process will not give you an adequate answer to any complex challenge.

To increase your awareness of what change might really be required, you need to explore more deeply different areas of the big picture — everything below the waterline of the iceberg ... plus the ocean around it. It is complex work that is best done with a diverse group of people. Systems thinking and systems sensing are next-level leadership skills.

The following are a few leadership tools to get you started:

1. **System Map:** A visual representation of the most important elements, and their relationships and interdependencies in the system, that are contributing to the problematic events you want to analyse. Very much an intellectual approach to systems thinking.

2. **Context-Sensing:** An experiential interaction with a system map. Practising a somatic approach to finding flow by system sensing.

3. **Mindset Check:** Consider your own and your stakeholders' mental models as reference points for what is influencing the system structures.

Leading in a system is a bit like sailing a small yacht. You have to know your start position first (mindset). Then you need to consider all elements and factors influencing your trip (map). Think of weather, waves, crew, etc. Ultimately, the skipper and navigator will use the map AND sense their way to the next way point (sensing).

How does this look in more detail?

System map

The quickest way to get started is just to do a simple system map, capturing the situation as you see it.

The parts of a system or space described below are important to consider when you explore any situation in a systemic way. Try to capture and reflect on as many of the following as possible.

1. Purpose
Systems start because of a purpose to serve. Purpose is a fundamental reference point and can change when the outside world changes. The purpose defines the system boundaries. You can create and lead a system by setting very clear intentions about what you want to achieve in any given situation. Your intention can create purpose and, thus, influence a system.

2. Elements
Elements are people, things, places or concepts that have a place in the system. They belong if they are connected to the purpose. Systems only care about wholeness, not morals or ethics. What are the core elements that can create an ideal basis for performance? If you do not know them, you cannot apply or share a better way.

3. Relationships
Relationships are connections between the elements. Obviously, these relationships can have different qualities that either support or hinder your chance of successfully creating positive impact. Most likely, there are many interdependencies to

consider and capture for further exploration. Feedback loops influence relationships and their qualities.

4. Patterns

What are you sensing is there, and what are you sensing is missing? What patterns are evolving over time? Can you notice behaviour patterns that might contribute to the current situation? If you are not aware, you are unable to gather crucial facts and subtle hints.

5. Order

Analysing the order of a system depends on how you look at the situation. Order can be defined by time (e.g. who came first) or hierarchy (e.g. where this role sat traditionally). Observe how you enter a system (e.g. first points of contact in an organisation).

6. Exchange

Give and take in relationships has to get to a balance after a while. The balance has to be perceived as fair by all sides.

7. Energy fields

Energy wants to flow through a system. If it is blocked, symptoms will show up as issues. Your body is your only tool to tune into an energy field. This is not an area for logic, but for sensing and feeling. You can't think your way through this flow. Going with what feels right is a challenge for many people, but it can be learned.

Drafting a system map will also provide more clarity on the level of complexity that you are facing. Your map might look like a snapshot in time. However, at the same time, it is good to remember that the real-world situation is never static and always evolving. As systems-thinking expert Peter Senge explained in an interview with the MIT Leadership Center: 'The systems viewpoint is generally oriented toward the long-term view. That's why delays and feedback loops are so important. In the short term, you can often ignore them; they're inconsequential. They only come back to haunt you in the long term.'

Try it out. Create a draft system map (see sample below) for your challenge and think through causes and effects at the various levels. How do physical places, like home, workplace, environment, country, planet, influence your wellbeing and performance as a leader and, thus, enable or hinder your ability to have a positive impact? What is the impact of technology, people and nature at every level?

There are many different ways to create these maps. There is no right or wrong way to do this. You can create an overview in whatever visual form suits your work and helps you to get more clarity on what is going on. If you are looking for some inspiration on how to do this, Google 'system map models'. There are plenty of examples.

Here is one way that I sometimes use with clients:

A SAMPLE SYSTEM MAP

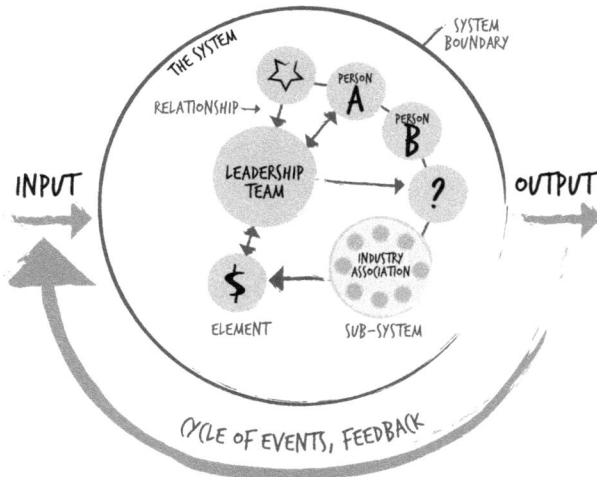

These maps mostly represent an intellectual approach — you think about a challenge, maybe discuss it with other people, and then run an iterative process to finetune and capture your perspectives.

Depending on whether your situation is pretty simple and clear or quite complicated, complex or even chaotic, your responses as a leader will need to match these different cause-and-effect context environments. David Snowden's Cynefin model provides a good framework for thinking about the requirements of decision making and leading. The first step is to achieve more awareness on what you notice right now in this moment. Start here with a system map and explore the Cynefin framework later.

Do not overcomplicate your system map. It can be a quick tool to expand your perspectives on a specific challenge and provide you with valuable insights that make it easier to define your next steps. Sometimes, a few Post-it Notes with names of people or tasks or issues, plus a few connecting lines on paper, are enough to generate new insights.

If you get stuck and are open to exploring a more intuitive approach, try the following.

Context-Sensing

Another systemic intelligence that we all possess, but don't often use, is our body's wisdom. Often, our bodies intuitively know where to look and what to do. This is what the next step is about — a somatic approach to exploring a system and its symptoms and challenges more deeply.

Fully capturing the bigger picture with all the facets of all the systems involved can be overwhelming at times. The more you discover, the more complex it becomes. One method I use with clients is stepping into the map. I invite them to explore the field.

Ideally, you would do this with at least one other person, but it can be a simple process that you can apply on your own as well. Write down the key elements of the system on paper or Post-it Notes. Lay these out on the ground in a way that represents the situation and all key connections in the system. This is your draft system map. Next, use your body's sensations to get fresh insights. Step onto the paper elements and/or walk in between them. Have a look around. Pause where it feels right for you. Sense into your body and listen to whatever thoughts come up for you. You might not hear the most logical thoughts, but by moving and changing perspectives, new ideas and solutions or next steps will come up — if you allow them to.

Not all methods can be described sufficiently with logic and words. Some have to be experienced. This is one of those. Trust the process, try it and experience for yourself what happens.

A more professional (and more thorough) version of this process is 'Systemic Constellation' work. Originally developed by German psychotherapist Bert Hellinger, a Systemic Constellation is a professionally facilitated process that reveals hidden dynamics in any system that humans are part of. Over the last few decades, Hellinger's work has been widely used and adapted by practitioners from a variety of application areas. The process uncovers resources that can bring resolution to internal issues within any relational system — natural, personal, professional or organisational. The facilitator invites participants to assume specific roles and places in a defined space. By being asked a set of well-researched questions, participants let new insights emerge from the field of the system which, ultimately, help them to create better solutions with less effort. Constellation work helps participants to explore relationships and connections in a new way and, thus, often helps to resolve even the most complex problem in a relatively short period of time.

Finally, to further increase your understanding of the whole situation, consider adding a mindset check.

Mindset check

Whatever event happens in your world, you will look at it through your lenses and make it mean something. A different person will look at the same event and give it a different meaning. Sometimes these meanings match, but often they do not. Our lenses were formed by different life experiences and education, and socialisation in different cultures. They include all our emotional baggage and intergenerational trauma. They are powerful filters of how to define a system.

 Thus, it is always worthwhile exploring what and how you and others think. We all create our own realities and definitions of how we experience specific context. Become aware of the place and perspective you and others operate from: the mindset. Remember my story with Uncle Max in the bush? What would you have answered when asked what you could see? Your answer gives you a reference point to determine your position and your level of awareness.

Reflecting on people's mindsets not only invites you to consider what framework they are operating in, but also indicates how much complexity and uncertainty a person can handle comfortably.

As nature is our ultimate life-giving system, it can be seen as the source or reference point for all other systems. Thus, the way a person views nature influences their leadership style and actions.

Check in with the following graphic to find out what type of nature mindset you have. It is normal to fluctuate between different levels and nothing is ever perfect. See it as a thought-starter for your leadership development and as a potential conversation point with your stakeholders.

THE HUMAN-NATURE CONNECTION...
INFLUENCES ON LEADERSHIP

HUMAN NATURE CONNECTION	HOW	RELATIONSHIP	LEADERSHIP
☺	BEYOND SENSORY DEEP MINDFUL CONNECTION, NATURE AS BASIS	ONENESS	ECO-SYSTEMIC
☺	ALL SENSES, IMMERSIVE	BIOPHILIC LOVER	COMMUNITY COLLABORATIVE
☺	CLOSE CONNECTION TOUCHING, SMELLING OR TASTING	BIOMIMICRY STUDENT	ACHIEVEMENT MOTIVATIONAL
☺	RELATIONAL, SEEING OR HEARING	RESOURCES BULLY	AUTHORITY HIERARCHICAL
☺	NO AWARENESS, MINDLESS CONNECTION	BACKDROP IGNORANT	EGO-FOCUS POWER

A potent, expansive question to ask when you get stuck explaining why certain issues are showing up in a system is: What other elements or connections might someone at the next level notice?

The higher the level of awareness, the more systemic, strategic and sustainable your mindset will become. All of this will make dealing with a 'VUCA' world a bit easier.

To sum it up: A system map can help you to better understand and navigate the spaces you are operating in. Context-sensing allows you to explore deeper layers. Understanding your and other people's mindsets helps explain why specific system structures were designed in their current way.

So, what could be the benefits of applying these processes?

EFFORTLESSLY NOTICING POTENTIAL POINTS OF IMPACT

Systems are everywhere. You are connected to them all the time. You never operate or lead in an isolated or empty space. Systems impact you, your team, your stakeholders, your organisation, your market — whether you want them to or not.

As a context-aware leader, you notice what is in your environment, clearly defining the elements and how they are connected to each other and you. You better understand the flow of life and how it is impacting you and your results.

Systems thinking and sensing help you to explore the whole of the system contributing to your challenges, enabling you to find optimal intervention points and be aware of blockages that might create symptoms and issues. You have more clarity on where and when to intervene to create change for positive impact.

Big-picture thinking (and sensing) means not only that you can see the forest AND the trees, but you also notice the rain, the soil, the sun, the people in the forest and other systems around them. You won't be surprised by the trees losing their leaves in autumn. You understand and anticipate some rhythm and timing happening in your space. You can align yourself and your work with it, thereby achieving what you want with less effort.

You get a good sense of where you belong and what you might be able to influence and impact positively — and where your influence

might be limited and you might need to nurture your patience and/
or acceptance. You don't waste your energy trying to push water
uphill, and instead see how it can flow around the hill and through
the next valley. You invest your energy in influencing where it matters most.

*With expanded insight, your decisions become
more sustainable and your effectiveness as
leader improves. You get more and more
aligned and in flow.*

THE ESSENCE

-CONTEXT-AWARENESS-

➢ Context-awareness is about noticing your connections to all systems around you by using all your senses. It is the awareness of what is impacting you, your team, your stakeholders and your results.

➢ Connecting and sensing the whole system gives you advanced and necessary information on how to optimally care for your and other people's wellbeing, and where and when to be a steward for the broader environment.

➢ One way to increase your context-awareness is to slow down mindfully, explore in detail what connections to the environments exist, and then draft a visual system map.

➢ Context-awareness improves your effectiveness as leader, makes your decisions more sustainable, and offers you a more expansive view of your place in the world. It can provide you with a deeper sense of belonging.

CHAPTER 8

STEWARDSHIP: CARE ABOUT AND FOR THE SYSTEM

'We don't inherit the Earth from our ancestors, we borrow it from our children.'

NATIVE AMERICAN PROVERB

	CONNECT	CARE	COMMIT
SELF	SELF AWARENESS	ENERGY MANAGEMENT	ACCOUNTABILTY
STAKEHOLDERS	COMMUNICATION	COLLABORATION	INFLUENCE
SYSTEMS	CONTEXT AWARENESS	**STEWARDSHIP**	IMPACT

You are now more aware of the context of your leadership actions. You have done a system map and can see more clearly what your 'iceberg' is made of. You see where and when it might make sense to intervene. And where it might not.

However, every day, we all still miss crucial elements of decision making. We often think too small and ignore the basis for all life: the planet we live on. Every system is part of the planetary and universal system. Every society, every ecosystem, every organisation, every workplace, every team, every home, every person. All are systems in a system. Accepting this makes taking on the role of caretaker of the world a logical next step.

Increasing your level of care will ultimately enable you to deliver better results.

Well-known and respected primatologist Jane Goodall, who worked with chimpanzees for many decades and then became a very outspoken environmental activist, has always seen the connections and influences of systems in and between our natural and human worlds. And all the problems that come with them.

In 2020, Goodall started to intensify her warnings. 'We have come to a turning point in our relationship with the natural world.' Jane believes that there is only a small window of opportunity to make drastic changes before we face disaster.

This is your opportunity to expand your circle of influence as a leader and contribute to the solutions — in whatever small way you can.

During the coronavirus pandemic in 2020, Jane Goodall voiced her belief that humans have (at least partly) contributed to the emergence of the COVID-19 virus. By over-exploiting the natural world, we created a situation that made it possible for the virus to jump from animals to humans. The Guardian newspaper reported that Jane Goodall warned that humanity will be 'finished' if we fail to drastically change our food systems in response to the coronavirus pandemic and the climate crisis.

Jane Goodall said that we have to do things differently. For example, by lifting people out of poverty, we can decrease the strong negative impact on the natural world. Poor people with no alternatives to feed their families cut down forests to survive, and in urban areas they

*will choose the cheapest food — no matter what harm its produc-
tion might have caused. By empowering these families to come out
of poverty, a positive impact on the environment is likely. Goodall
wants wealthy people to stop buying from companies that use factory
farming or cause harm to the environment in any way.*

The Guardian *said of her appeal: 'One of the lessons learned from
this crisis is that we must change our ways. Scientists warn that to
avoid future crises, we must drastically change our diets and move to
plant-rich foods. For the sake of the animals, planet and the health
of our children.'*

Changing your diet is a small, very personal contribution you can
make to show your care. At work, your influence and potential
impact might be even bigger. Any social change empowering people
to make better food choices adds more positive impact. Integrating
social and environmental sustainability at the core of your business
strategy increases your positive impact.

Given the fact that a fully intact ecosystem was designed to function
sustainably for long periods, I suggest that we take nature as a role
model for our own actions. Nature can help us decide which actions
are beneficial for people and planet.

We can refer to the natural world as a basis for all living systems'
design, including humans. Thus, the following principles can help
you to understand how systems work and where to intervene for
change.

These seven universal principles are reference points for you when
deciding on your next actions as steward. They give you added perspectives for your system map and may help explain specific events.

1. **Interconnectedness**: Everything is connected.
2. **Circularity**: Waste is food.
3. **Cooperation**: Competition creates loss.

4. **Rhythm** and timing: All things grow and decline.
5. **Change**: Everything changes all the time.
6. **Polarity** and correspondence: There are always two sides.
7. **Diversity** and optimisation: Differences support growth.

Are you including these principles in all of your work? How much do you know about them? How well can you use them on a daily basis? The more you expand your skills in these areas, the easier it will be to navigate a VUCA world of volatility, uncertainty, complexity and ambiguity.

Ultimately, your role as steward and wise leader is to channel the world's natural flow for performance and wellbeing. That is a big task. Are you up for this?

Why would it make sense for you to consider expanding your circle of influence and care for all relevant systems around you?

CARING MORE OPENS UP NEW PATHWAYS TO MORE POSITIVE IMPACT

As a good steward, you care for a system that ultimately connects back to you and your team or stakeholders. This is especially true for connecting and caring for your natural environments. You take all opportunities to create ideal conditions for optimal wellbeing and high performance for all people involved.

In 1991, American outdoor clothing and equipment company Patagonia had a sales and cashflow crisis. Their founder, Yvon Chouinard, was looking for ways to do business differently. He did not want to adopt the contemporary model of corporate America. Due to his experiences as a climber, surfer, kayaker and fly fisherman, he had learned to live his life fairly simply and in tune with nature. He had

STEWARDSHIP: CARE ABOUT AND FOR THE SYSTEM

started to notice the increasingly degraded state of the environment. This led him to choose to eat lower on the food chain and reduce his consumption. While taking part in risky sports, he also learned the principle: 'Never exceed your limits to stay safe.'

Yvon Chouinard wanted to bring some of these insights to his struggling business. He took inspiration from the Native American Iroquois people and their seven-generation planning as a model for his version of stewardship and sustainability. The Iroquois used as part of their decision process a person who represented the seventh generation in the future. To help Patagonia survive its crisis, Yvon wanted the company to make all of its decisions as though they would be in business for a hundred years. Patagonia would only grow at a rate that they could sustain for that long. Yvon started to teach the new philosophy to every employee and also set up a few different advisor circles with people of diverse backgrounds. Over the next few years, Patagonia started to thrive again and became an inspiration for many other businesses that are searching for their own version of stewardship and sustainability.

Patagonia is driven by its high-quality standards and classic design principles. Today, it can be seen as one of the most environmentally sustainable companies in its market. Yvon also noticed the decline of many societal institutions that had been providing ethical and social guidance to people. He felt that this lack of an ethical centre could partly be filled by companies that show their employees and customers that they understand their own ethical responsibilities, and thereby help employees and customers respond to their own. The quest for better social sustainability and activism became even more important over time. In 2001, the 'one per cent for the planet' initiative was created. It is an alliance of businesses that contribute at least one per cent of their net annual sales to selected environmental organisations. From time to time, Patagonia also takes an activist stand for different environmental and social issues. Patagonia defines stewardship very broadly.

Today, no business or organisation is exempt from these social and environmental challenges. The solutions are all available; what is missing is the awareness and willingness to lead in different ways.

The caring aspect of stewardship opens
up new pathways to more effective and
positive impact on people and planet.

It takes courage, persistence, knowledge and good influencing skills to practise good stewardship and make a positive difference.

For stewardship to successfully create sustainable change, you need to also be in tune with the natural flow of life and understand all relevant systems around you. The context-awareness that you gain by applying systems thinking and sensing helps you to explore the whole system contributing to your challenges. It enables you to identify optimal intervention points and be aware of blockages.

Systems can be hard to understand and navigate. Thus, many people choose just to focus on selected snippets. Unfortunately, this limited perspective wastes a lot of energy, time and money — often with negative consequences.

It doesn't have to be this way. There have been countless generations of wisdom keepers before us, and it is very possible to tap into large parts of their knowledge today. All that is needed to start improvements is an open mind, curiosity and collaboration. Stewardship takes a holistic and systemic approach to optimising care for systems.

However, we have forgotten some of the basic skills that are necessary for practising good stewardship, and they are no longer taught. These skills include navigation, patience, caring for the land, understanding time/rhythm, reading and interacting with nature, channelling energy flows and seeing the whole. A fully nature-connected mindset, as described earlier, is often missing.

Not knowing how to be in and with nature, or how to work with it with respect and reciprocity, has led to the development of activities and products that are slowly destroying planet and humanity. It is a dysfunctional relationship that can't be repaired by technology or science alone. We have to go back to what came before and integrate this into our work today. Investing time in some basic activities that create a firsthand experience and knowledge of nature can help us to rebuild the connection.

Approaching work with a stewardship mindset will make you feel more connected, engaged and satisfied when delivering a positive impact.

All of this newly rediscovered knowing will impact your decision making and, therefore, your daily actions as an effective, wise leader. Working towards an environmentally sustainable, socially just and economically viable world requires you to take a systemic view more often.

So, what does stewardship look like in this context?

STEWARDS PRACTISE CARE FOR THE WHOLE SYSTEM

Historically, stewardship was defined as an ethic *that embodies the responsible planning and management of* resources. Later, this was extended to the acceptance or assignment of responsibility to shepherd and safeguard the valuables of others. These 'others' can come from other places or times, as in the Iroquois' seven-generation principle.

In this sense, stewardship is the careful and responsible management of something entrusted to one's care.

This idea is perfectly expressed in the quote by Native American Chief Seattle, who said: 'We do not inherit the Earth from our ancestors — we borrow it from our children.'

To fully practise this way of working, you need a mindset of being in service to the greater good and big picture. You need awareness, knowledge, intuition, wisdom and a focus on action.

Ben Cohen and Jerry Greenfield are a great example of this. They founded Ben & Jerry's in 1978. Even though the company 'just' produced ice cream, frozen yoghurt and sorbets, Ben and Jerry demonstrated great care and activism for their whole supply chain and all communities they operated in. They are an inspiring example of how stewardship can work in all industries and markets. Their brand grew so strong that even after they sold it to Unilever in 2000, the core philosophies and ethics of stewardship were still practised — and continue to be practised today. The Ben & Jerry's way of doing business is driven by using the power of their ingredients and purchasing decisions to inspire change; using their manufacturing processes to further environmental, social and economic justice; and practising a variety of 'giving back' activities to support social change. The founders are no longer actively involved in the business, but still try to create change for the better by getting involved in environmental and social activism. Their stewardship approach for the greater good didn't stop when they sold the company.

For today's leaders, stewardship is about actively caring about and for the whole system — however far your circle of influence reaches.

A wise leader who practises stewardship puts service over self-interest. They look at the bigger picture and have sufficient knowledge to understand how their context-systems work. They focus on delivering results that are aligned with the needs, principles and balance of the systems around them. Sometimes this can mean preserving the status quo, and other times it can mean nudging for change.

Stewardship can be creation,
conservation or renewal.

By adding something, conserving the current status or cutting back on things, you act a bit like a gardener — that is, one who follows permaculture or biodynamic gardening practices instead of quick-fix, short-term planting. Real stewardship aims to act on what is needed to care for a system to make sure that positive impact results are sustainably possible in the long run.

How would you do this?

ACT FROM A PLACE OF WISDOM AND SERVICE

By practising context-awareness, you go through the process of locating, connecting to and accepting all systems relevant to your challenge. Accepting means seeing things as they currently appear to you. You notice that they can be perfect in being imperfect. This type of awareness is all about BEING connected with the systems.

Stewardship now means active DOING. You explore what needs change to make it better and what can stay as is.

A number of dramatic events at the beginning of 2020 were a wake-up call to do business differently: bushfires in Australia and other places, accelerating climate-change problems in many countries, severe droughts, the COVID-19 pandemic and social unrest, including the Black Lives Matter rallies. Different people and organisations responded in different ways — coming from different levels of awareness and curiosity. Sometimes, what you care about or for can be quite divisive for your stakeholders. However, as a leader, deciding next steps based on your values and purpose is important for ultimately creating change and positive impact.

Dollar Shave Club, a brand owned by Unilever, did just that during the Black Lives Matter protests and made a promise to do more. Their core business is selling razors in monthly subscription packages. Their CEO, Michael Dubin, and his team showed leadership in their circle of influence. By publicly stating on social media that they were planning to learn more about racism and would endeavour to eradicate it in their business, they hoped to inspire other businesses to take a stand and do more of what is in their circle of influence.

Not all of the Dollar Shave Club customers liked the company's point of view and some said they would never again buy from them, as they didn't want to be lectured about their moral shortcomings. Some customers on Facebook said things like, 'Just sell me razor blades and keep your mouth shut about political issues. I don't want to be lectured by you and will never buy from you again.' But these people were probably not the right customers in the first place, as they likely didn't care where the materials for their blades came from or whether child labour, slavery or other unethical methods were used to produce them.

However, there was another group who was attracted to the values that the company demonstrated. I do not know the ultimate outcome, but I guess that Dollar Shave Club at least kept their customer numbers high, and possibly grew their customer base. The point is that they showed Wise Leadership by caring for the whole system they operate in: all levels of supply chain and all areas where they do business and everyone with whom they do business. In some ways, they started a form of conscious activism in their business. We will have to wait and see how this will evolve.

Before you start acting as a steward, decide if you are willing and able to change and shift parts of the systems. For what parts do you want to take full responsibility? It is crucial to recognise whether you are acting pro-actively in your circle of influence, or whether you are wasting energy by being reactive in your larger circle of concern.

Once you have clarity around your position, you are ready to enter an iterative process of stewardship. Try the following steps:

1. Assess
2. Act
3. Adapt

What does this care as steward look like?

1. Assess

Your guiding question to explore here is:

What knowledge and wisdom do you have
and/or need to make better decisions
to choose a relevant path of action
that expands your positive impact?

Know where you can be effective. Consider Stephen Covey's concept of the circle of influence versus the circle of concern. Covey taught us that there are many topics in your larger circle of concern, but you can only actively work on the issues in your smaller circle of influence. By taking full responsibility and being proactive in your circle of influence, you can slowly expand your field of positive impact. You live your life from a place of trust and choice, not fear and blame. Sounds very logical and simple, and yet I know from many, many coaching conversations, it is a concept that is frequently forgotten and causes a great deal of stress.

There is a danger during this phase: The focus on knowledge and expertise often brings us to transactional relationships where people assume that they have all the important answers. Wisdom comes with more humility, and the knowledge that all the right answers might not be readily available. Wisdom is trusting that proven principles, lived values, slowly acquired experience and intuition will lead to the emergence of sustainable solutions. Its focus is often on mindful, respectful and transformational relationships.

We have come to a point in history where we can access data, information and knowledge quite easily. There are many experts with a lot of knowledge around. However, often, the wisdom of how to apply this knowledge for the greater good has been lost. Many experts know a lot on the intellectual level, but have never had any in-depth, sensory experience of the systems for which they design change solutions. Your task as a wise leader is to refer back to some timeless, proven and basic principles.

Immerse yourself and your team in the system. Take time to visit, listen and observe all elements and their interactions. So-called field visits are necessary if you are not already deeply engaged in the system that you have decided to care for. If you can't organise a direct experience, find a vicarious one. All of this might take some time, which is better invested the more complex your tasks are. We need more local expertise with a global view. Many larger organisations still have global views on local challenges. Too often, leaders who are not part of the system they want to change make the important decisions. To be effective, you have to be part of the system. Then you will know what needs to be done to care for your context and the spaces you are in.

Having the patience and openness to wait, and not act immediately, requires a higher level of awareness and maturity as leader. It is the recognition that inaction can have a higher value than action, that having 'enough' might be more satisfying than creating or acquiring 'more.'

An assessment from a place of wisdom leads to better decisions on how to act.

2. Act

Your guiding question to explore:

> *What actions will create alignment, care and/*
> *or change and ultimately provide you with*
> *heightened clarity on which path to take?*

Some of the specific actions might already have become clear to you when you worked on your context-awareness. Mapping and exploring your system by thinking it through and sensing it often provides powerful insights that can lead to immediate action steps. The assess step is then a valuable check-in phase to finetune your actions to become more effective.

> *For most actions to be useful, they need to*
> *happen at the right time and in the right place.*

The different energetic qualities of time and place are not always taken into consideration when designing a plan of action. For example, when working in remote teams spread across different time zones and global locations, each person will bring a different energy to virtual meetings — some are in a morning mood and feeling fresh; some are closing off their daily work late in the evening and feeling stale. Teams might be in countries with very different seasons, weather and political realities. All of this influences your systemic work and outcomes. If meetings are always rushed and only focus on tasks, relationship problems will pop up at some stage.

How will you as the steward for this system lead this project? How can you create alignment? Who will decide where change is needed? Place-based leadership would utilise more local expertise and self-organisation. Maybe your role as steward is to step aside and share the leadership.

What else is worthwhile considering around the topic of 'time'? Short-term, long-term, quick, slow ... in most cases, care cannot be rushed. You need to be deliberate and mindful, and listen to what action wants to emerge as the most useful one. In today's economy and society, action-orientation is highly valued. Busy is a common word. However, often, it is better to do nothing and go back to some simple, timeless principles to inform your next activity.

Slowing down is a different perspective, perfectly expressed in the quote by Lao Tzu: 'Nature does not hurry, yet everything is accomplished.'

This accomplishment is often like a dance: You move forwards and backwards and constantly adjust your body movements. It is the same for stewardship.

Not all actions as steward will be successful. Most of the time, adaptation is needed and normal.

3. Adapt

Your guiding question to explore:

What reflections and changes will give
you increased confidence to be on a
good path to positive impact?

All that is necessary to say here is: Go back to the principles of circularity, rhythm and change. Nature operates with many different types of feedback loops. As a system, it is always interested in wholeness and balance. Your task as a steward is to listen for feedback to adapt whatever is not working in the first round.

Stay in the flow of the system and become 'unbelievably adaptive.'

Never believe that you know the answer to everything. Stay curious and be at ease with what is. Learn to stay at ease with uncertainty. It is all natural and you are not alone in this challenge.

If you stay long enough in this re-iterative process, your stewardship will become more and more valuable and ultimately pay off for you and your cause and work.

What will you be left with?

BECOME A STRATEGIC INFLUENCER AND A FORCE FOR GOOD

As a steward, you know what counts. You are very aware of where, when and how to invest your time, energy and effort to create systemic change. Having the big picture in mind, you know what systems you are part of and how to care for them. Other people intuitively, and often unconsciously, notice this. In many ways, you can be a role model and guiding light when situations become very unclear and challenging. You are someone who not only can see the forest for the trees, but also knows how to care for the forest to keep it healthy, beautiful and thriving.

By exploring timeless wisdom and its principles more intensely, you build more awareness of and capacity for how systems work. You know how nature has designed living systems and how you can use this knowledge for the benefit of all people you connect with at work. You can notice parallels and commonalities between different types of systems. This helps you to design action plans that are open to adaptation. You practise Wise Leadership.

Over time, you will develop an increased sensitivity to energy flows in systems. By allowing these different perspectives, you will increase your chances of achieving great results that ultimately deliver the positive impact you set out to create in the beginning.

Stewardship makes you a strategic influencer and a force for good. Within your circle of influence, it can grow your reputation as a wise and well-respected leader who really cares. The care factor will spill over into other relationships as well. When people notice that a leader genuinely cares for people and planet, they respond differently to you. Coming from a place of service and wisdom, not selfishness and a focus on cold data, is something the world needs more of right now. Approaching work with a stewardship mindset will make you feel more connected, engaged and satisfied when delivering a positive impact.

Next, we will be exploring how this positive impact can be measured and how you can commit to it.

THE ESSENCE

—STEWARDSHIP—

➤ Stewardship is about actively caring about and for the whole system. It is an important part of the type of Wise Leadership that works towards an environmentally sustainable, socially just and economically viable world.

➤ By caring for the system, you ultimately care for yourself and other people. You create ideal conditions for optimal wellbeing and high performance.

➤ By acquiring deeper knowledge of the systemic context of your leadership challenges, you can better decide whether to navigate the systems by getting aligned and in flow or influencing changes where they are needed to improve positive impact outcomes.

➤ Stewardship makes you a strategic influencer and a force for good. Within your circle of influence, it can grow your reputation as a wise and well-respected leader who really cares.

CHAPTER 9

IMPACT: DEFINE WHAT SUCCESS IS

'I long to accomplish great and noble tasks, but it is my chief duty to accomplish humble tasks as though they were great and noble ... The world is moved along, not only by the mighty shoves of its heroes, but also by the aggregate of the tiny pushes of each honest worker.'

(HELEN KELLER)

	CONNECT	CARE	COMMIT
SELF	SELF AWARENESS	ENERGY MANAGEMENT	ACCOUNTABILTY
STAKEHOLDERS	COMMUNICATION	COLLABORATION	INFLUENCE
SYSTEMS	CONTEXT AWARENESS	STEWARDSHIP	**IMPACT**

'I don't know whether my work actually makes a positive impact, or not.'

Michael was frustrated. He felt like all his passion for 'making the world a better place' did not show up anywhere in his work in a tangible way. At the same time he felt a sense of urgency, as climate change was an increasingly problematic factor in his market.

First, I thought that his question was a bit unexpected. I had been coaching him only for a brief period but knew that in his role as sustainability leader in a medium-sized business, he was leading several change initiatives that sounded like they would create a huge positive impact. Nevertheless, he could not see any impacts and, more importantly, couldn't feel that he was living true to his purpose.

I had a similar experience with another client a few years earlier when I was facilitating a sustainability innovation project. A company in the beverage market wanted to explore whether sustainable wine might be an interesting addition to their product portfolio. This was very forward thinking, as there was hardly anything sustainable on the wine shelves in larger bottle shops. But when we started the project, it turned out that none of the leaders actually had any idea of what sustainable wine actually is. Is it less waste with the packaging, less emissions from production, better nutrients and soil, better farming practices, better work conditions for vineyard workers, or what?

They also had no idea of any impact assessments. They just had the inkling that this would be an interesting, new market segment and that it would be great to do something positive for the environment. Although the project team loved the increased focus on sustainability, they doubted that their work would really make a huge impact on the rest of the portfolio. They had no idea what positive impact would look like.

I have seen these types of client scenarios repeating themselves again and again over the years.

What is missing, most of the time, is the big picture and a strategically integrated view of what an organisation's impact on the environment, society and all its stakeholders really is — over time and in different places.

This in combination with an unclear purpose leaves people confused about whether their work is creating change and positive impact or not. They are becoming frustrated and impatient.

Success is often not clearly defined
because there is little awareness or focus
on how everything — an organisation's
impact on the environment, society and
all its stakeholders — is connected.

FEELING SUCCESSFUL
CREATES MOMENTUM

If you are passionate about changing the world for the better, it can be difficult to notice whether your work is having the intended impact. Better understanding the nuances of what actually effects change makes a big difference to your sense of purpose and satisfaction at work.

For system impact, the definition of success is really important. Leaders who fail to define the impact they want are getting frustrated because, subconsciously, they want to have a really big positive impact. And this means they might fail to notice or see the small, incremental steps that lead to that big impact.

In their day-to-day life, they're not really seeing that they're making progress or achieving anything. This is because they never really defined the small steps or details of what make up the bigger picture of the impact they want to see. They might have a big vision, but they have never really defined the more specific details of the vision and how to get there. If they do this, ultimately, with each step towards their goal, they would feel a bit more successful. And each little bit of success leads to a sense of being truly impactful.

*A focus on positive impact as an end
result can cause a lot of unnecessary
stress and frustration during the process
of delivering it. You have to manage your
own expectations of what success is.*

Success takes many, many small steps.

HOW MANY DINGOES?

*In 2007, I walked part of the Larapinta Trail in Central Australia. At
the start, the weather was challenging. It rained for days and many
sections of the trail were flooded. We got stuck in a small Aboriginal
community called Hermannsburg, and spent our days camping in
the historic buildings that had no doors. Think of damp, cold, windy
nights sleeping on mats, joined by a few local dingoes. Not exactly the
family holiday we had envisioned. However, it became a successful
learning journey.*

*We learned some fun things, for example, that some Indigenous people
jokingly measure temperature degrees by the number of dingoes they
want to have sleeping next to them (like most dogs, they are quite
warming). We learned how to make fire — from damp wood. We
learned how to get along with a very diverse group of about twenty
people — in a small space with one(!) bathroom. We learned to listen
to the rain and wind ... and to each other.*

*When we eventually started the hike, some people were very eager
to get to our next destination — constantly asking our Aboriginal
guide: 'How much further is it?' His answer: 'Not long.' Half an hour
later, same question and ... same answer. After a while, everyone
succumbed to just being in the moment, and enjoying the landscape
and each other's company. We successfully navigated some muddy
tracks, flooded creeks and gorges, slippery rocks and fallen trees. We*

were in awe when stopping at some breathtaking vistas and learning about tiny sacred sites and their meaning.

It was a successful trip — despite the rain, the cold and the ongoing discomfort. Every person left Alice Springs (where our trip ended) a richer person. Richer in new perspectives and insights, and richer in life-long memories and deeper relationships. The time spent exposed to wild nature had shown us new dimensions of what it means to be a human being. It taught us patience, acceptance, humility. We learned to listen more deeply and ask fewer questions.

Success is a feeling, not a destination.

The success of our journey was not only that we arrived safe and sound in Alice Springs. The real success was the proud feeling of going through adversity and challenges to come out on the other side as a more holistic person. No one had thought about that impact when we started our trip.

It was an unintended positive side effect. These positive impacts happen. However, there are many reasons why it makes sense to explore and define successful impacts before you start any new venture. Some clarity about your destination helps.

A focus on what type of impact you want to create as leader can provide inspiration and direction to all people you work with.

Your impact vision creates a sense of being on purpose every step along the way —even when you have to take a detour. It keeps you focused on what is important for you.

IMPACT EQUALS CHANGE

Measuring your impact is one way of capturing the success of change you create in the world. Your leadership decisions and actions create outcomes and results that have strong effects on someone or something.

Impact is your effect on people or planet — while remembering at the same time that you are impacted by them as well. It is a never-ending circle.

Your energy flows where your attention goes. This means that whatever you focus on will attract your efforts and action and, thus, ultimately create results and impact in the area that you pre-defined. Therefore, thinking deeply about the impact you want to create is also a type of energy management — for yourself and the people who work with you.

Successful impact needs a broader, different definition from the one we currently see. It is often limited to your outward actions, where you are doing something to or for someone or something else. This definition neglects the 'incoming' impact.

In an earlier chapter, I shared the principles of living systems with you. Because everything on our planet is connected, we receive many benefits from ecosystems around us. They keep humanity alive. Ecosystems can only successfully deliver on this task if they are healthy themselves. Right now, they are not, and humanity is suffering in many different ways. Our impact balance sheet as a whole is negative. For many leaders who are aware of the dimension of the crisis, the task of coming back to positive impacts feels overwhelming. Quite often, they cannot even appreciate their small positive contributions along the way. A renewed perspective on purpose is needed.

*Thus, environmental and social considerations
need to be part of every leadership decision.*

In an ideal case, they would be part of the core business strategy, not just add-on strategies.

Achieving meaningful measurement of impact is a complex process. You have to be aware that you are not the only player in the system who is creating change. Thus, not all of the results are necessarily caused by your leadership. Some can only be achieved in collaboration and cooperation with other partners.

Before defining the measurement criteria, it would be good to consider that there are six different types of impact:

1. **Direct / indirect**
   Do your activities have a direct or indirect effect on people and planet?

2. **Intended / unintended**
   Is the change only showing intended effects or are there unintended side-effects as well?

3. **Positive / negative**
   Your impact can be constructive, destructive or neutral.

4. **Quantitative / qualitative**
   Not every impact can be measured with numerical data, and if you use numbers, you should also tell the stories behind the data. Sometimes, anecdotal evidence is a first indicator that you might be on the right path.

5. **Different time horizons**
   What time horizon are you taking into consideration — short term, medium term, long term, next seven generations?

6. Different places
What locality do you focus on — local, national, international, global, universal? What is your circle of influence? Where is your impact more of a contribution to a larger whole?

So, how would you use these perspectives to define what impact you are committing your leadership to?

CLARIFYING DESIRED IMPACT SUCCESS

We are not always fully aware whose success benchmark we are working towards and WHY it is important. Become clear about where expectations originally came from — did you create them for yourself or did some external source ask you to meet these goals?

Thus, it is essential for your wellbeing, and your team's, to check what your measurement of success is. Success needs very subjective, individual measurement; otherwise, it will negatively impact your wellbeing and with that — your performance.

I invite you to reflect on the following perspectives:

1. Process vs. Outcome

Are you only interested in the shortest way to achieve a specific outcome, or do you observe and enjoy all the steps that get you there? There is nothing wrong with the former, and it is not better to do the latter. Still, it is worthwhile to be clear on your personal style.

The awareness of what you are
focusing on is essential knowledge
of how you are creating impact.

2. Expectations vs. Acceptance

The biggest cause for stress, personally and in the workplace, is the gap between our expectations and reality. When you are totally fixed on a specific expected outcome (which is always in the future), slight deviations (in the present moment) will cause you stress and discomfort. Decide whether it is worth the effort and stress.

The acceptance of current realities often provides new perspectives for solutions as soon as you relax into the challenge.

3. Comparing yourself with others

We constantly look at our lives and results in comparison to others, which can be very dangerous for our self-worth. As we never know the full story of the other person, we might compare our Chapter 13 with their Chapter 31. You should only compare yourself with yourself. Consider how you can use others' Chapter 31 as inspiration to find different ways of doing things on your path as leader.

Your capacity for impact is unique and naturally limited. Comparison kills joy.

By consciously defining and communicating what successful impact looks and feels like in different timeframes and places, you are also pro-actively choosing your leadership brand. You define what you stand for and where you want to take your work to. It helps you determine how you show up as a leader.

The more awareness you have about the benchmarks you are working towards, the easier it becomes to stay on track and be patient and satisfied with incremental progress.

You might be driven by short-term KPIs that were given to you by your organisation or striving to leave a personal legacy for the world. Emotional engagement can be quite different for these two.

Make sure you know exactly
what really matters to you.

The following questions can help you explore what impact you desire to create. Defining the impact is an iterative, non-linear process. You might start with one definition, test it out and then decide to either finetune it or create a new one.

Here are a few areas to explore and test out.

1. Consider your WHY

Check your values and purpose to become clear about WHY you want to create this specific impact. Your intention matters.

2. Define your WHAT

Go back to the six different types of impact. Some of these perspectives will be relevant for your own definition.

Locate your desire to create positive impact on one of the system maps we discussed earlier in this book. Place and time are important considerations that show your impact beyond the here and now. That is why impact sometimes feels a bit distant. There will be many, many different ways of measuring your impact. The following are just a few examples and thoughts for your consideration:

PLACE
Explore and note in what places your impact might show up.

Planetary level
Impact on nature and ecosystems. Measurements include waste, biodiversity, carbon footprints, water footprints, Sustainable Development Goals.

Societal level
Social justice, economic inclusion, diversity. Measurements include indicators like social impact index, GDP vs. GNH (Gross National Happiness Index in Bhutan).

Company level
Wellbeing, economic and sustainability performance. Measurements include internal KPIs, Green Star Ratings, BCorp impact assessment.

Individual level
Personal impact assessment and legacy. Measurements include your own subjective judgements, personal perception of seeing other people change or receiving feedback.

TIME
There are three different timeframes to consider. Start from the long-term, big-picture view.

Long-term — your end of life
Visualise the legacy you want by writing your own eulogy — include your values and purpose.

Medium-term — 1-3 years
Get clarity on your purpose and the next steps you want to take to fully live it. External benchmarks, like Green Star, Living Building Challenge, UN-SDG.

Short-term — 1-6 months
KPIs, project measures.

Your definition of impact will largely define your intentions and how you show up in any system. A positive vision instils hope and empowers action through people following you.

SUCCESSFUL IMPACT

It is a deep-seated, innate human need — wanting to contribute positively to other people and the larger environment. Having a positive impact, and, thus, leaving a positive legacy, is on the 'to-achieve' list of many leaders. Yet, not many take the time to truly reflect on what success would look and feel like for them.

Exploring and defining what positive impact is for you and why it really matters to you will increase your awareness of what success is for you. You become liberated from just having to unconsciously follow outside expectations. Your new freedom of choice might not always be easy, but it puts you back in the driver seat of what type of leader you want to be.

Noticing and accepting that not all of your impact will be immediately visible and tangible will help you to stay patient and calm when events do not play out in your favour. These might just be a temporary setback that, put into the bigger picture, might even have some positives. Many, many small steps create big impact — eventually. Just keep going.

By investing time in your definition of what positive impact is, you will learn a lot about all the systems you are part of and where your circle of influence ends — for now. This creates more awareness of how any context can support or hinder your results, your wellbeing and your performance. It also becomes more obvious where you can invest time and energy to push the boundaries, and where it might make sense to do nothing.

*Impact definition is part of managing
your and other people's energy.*

Knowing what impact you desire will give you and all the people you lead a clear direction on where to focus your energies to create successes that you can actually feel and enjoy. Frustrations are reduced. You will all have higher levels of satisfaction with work achievements.

A focus on positive impact will make a valuable contribution to your legacy. It brings you one step closer to becoming a wise leader who channels the world's energy and flow with the aim to be a force for good.

To avoid more suffering in the world, wise leaders need to take a more conscious approach to what they stand for and what type of positive impact they want to create. If you want to contribute to a shift that ensures people and planet are not only surviving but thriving, remember that all your choices and every decision create an impact.

*A renewed focus on the natural world
as a source of energy is vital for your
sustainable success. It supports you to
successfully create positive impact for you,
for other people and for the whole world.*

THE ESSENCE

-IMPACT-

➤ Impact is the result of leadership. It can be constructive, destructive or neutral. In an ideal case, it is about committing to and achieving positive impact for the whole system. It can be a measurement of success and be part of your legacy.

➤ A focus on what type of impact you create as leader provides inspiration and direction to all people you work with. Not all leaders are equally aware of what the impacts of their actions are. To avoid more suffering in the world, wise leaders need to take a more conscious approach to what they stand for. A renewed focus on the natural world as a source of energy is vital.

➤ By consciously defining and communicating what success looks and feels like in different timeframes and places, you are also proactively choosing your leadership brand. It will largely define your intentions and how you show up in any system. A positive vision instils hope in and empowers action by the people following you.

➤ You, others and the whole system become more balanced and start to thrive. You appreciate and enjoy the alignment and flow you create. A focus on positive impact will make a valuable contribution to your legacy.

.

PART 3 – SYSTEMS

SEEDS FOR
THOUGHTS

I invite you to take some time for reflection and explore new perspectives on ... **leading in SYSTEMS.**

1. What helps you to notice more of your context?

2. What do you really care about in your environments?

3. Which three daily habits would make a huge difference in terms of considering all parts and the whole?

4. How do you define success?

5. What are you committed to changing when creating positive impact?

CONCLUSION

WISE LEADERSHIP MAKES YOU NATURALLY SUCCESSFUL

'Everything will be all right in the end ... if it's not all right then it's not yet the end.'

(ATTRIBUTED TO MANY SOURCES)

Wise leaders change the world for the better — one small step at a time and in their circle of influence, which can be very small or quite large. You can be one of them. Wise leaders can be any age, work in any industry or type of organisation, and be experts in any topic. When you meet them, you will notice a type of positive energy radiating from them. They think, talk and act differently. Their visions are very holistic and inclusive. They are highly aware of their environments and other people. They show they care, and they are committed to 100 per cent personal responsibility. I have met many of them. They inspired me to write this book. One of them is Leila Fourie.

Leila works in an industry that usually gets quite mixed reviews in terms of its reputation, trustworthiness and contribution to sustainability and social justice. Leila's business career in consulting, investment banking, retail banking and capital markets spans more than twenty years. Her diverse experience was acquired in some of

South Africa's, Australia's and the USA's leading companies in these fields. In October 2019, she was appointed the CEO of the Johannesburg Stock Exchange (JSE).

When Leila is not working, she spends time in nature — in the bush and on mountains, hiking, climbing and mountaineering. Climate change is a profoundly important topic for her. Family and friends are high on her values list and she is genuinely interested in the well-being of all people. Thus, social issues, like the ones that her country of birth, South Africa, faces, motivate her to use every power she has to mobilise change.

Leila has been very vocal about her understanding that privilege comes with great responsibility. She has three objectives for the JSE that very much represent her thinking in general:

1. *Co-creation and partnerships for growth;*
2. *Rebuilding trust and resilience; and*
3. *Nation-building and contributing to the national agenda.*

She further desires that the JSE become a leader in sustainable development. Even during the COVID-19 crisis, Leila and her team found many ways to collaborate with a variety of stakeholders and stay true to these goals.

In addition to her CEO role, Leila is co-chairing the UN Secretary-General's Global Investors for Sustainable Development Alliance: a group of thirty global CEOs of the largest institutions of their kind — committed to urging the broader business sector to better integrate Sustainable Development Goals into their core business models, introducing long-term performance metrics, accelerating company disclosure, and reporting on social and environmental issues. They have also pledged to advocate for a co-ordinated international approach to financial regulation and encourage ratings agencies to incorporate sustainable development considerations into their decision making.

All of Leila's activities are strategically focused and aligned to create win-win solutions with maximum positive impact. It is a challenging task and she knows that she can only deliver on her vision when she is well and supported.

She realised early on that a lot of her thinking came from her upbringing. Her approach to life and work is influenced by the lessons she learned from her mother and grandmother. She watched them and listened to what they were saying. Among other things, they taught her imagination, curiosity, endurance, mental fortitude in the face of adversity, and forgiveness. Later on, Leila had many male mentors and nowadays is mentoring women from all walks of life. She believes that as businesswomen, we have an obligation to use our privilege to support others — and the planet.

Leila admits that she has not always been the most confident person. She had to teach herself to become more confident and wishes that she had more confidence when she was younger. This translated into her mountain climbing ventures, where she learned to trust and have confidence step by step. She got through some very tough situations. When climbing Mt Vincent in Antarctica, she was faced with the difficult decision of whether she should go to the summit or not. Ultimately, she was able to get to the summit despite her doubts and physical limitations. It became a defining moment for her.

Leila advocates that technology advancement is needed to solve our most pressing problems. The success of this approach will depend on the culture a leader creates. Change in organisations has to move from 'people knowing a lot' to 'people learning a lot.' This will be one of the differentiators for innovation. A mindset of learning, the so-called Growth Mindset, is absolutely key for this.

The more Leila travelled and worked in other countries and cultures, the more her way of thinking shifted over the years. Often, she had to embrace new ways of thinking.

One quote that inspired her to get through all sorts of tough situations is from Nelson Mandela:

'There is no passion to be found playing small — in settling for a life that is less than the one you are capable of living.'

Leila always asks people, 'You have about 20,000 breaths a day ... what are you doing during these breaths? Are you making something with your life?'

So, what are your next steps?

I started writing this book because I had met too many leaders who were very passionate about changing the world for the better, but who easily got overwhelmed and stressed by the amount of work to be done to inspire and implement even tiny improvements. They were facing many 'difficult' stakeholders and often found it challenging to see the big picture and the foundations that carry us all. They were burning the candle at both ends — often forgetting to take proper care of themselves. You might have been one of those leaders.

Which new insights from the book might help you to achieve more with less stress?

The world wants you to be your best. We need more (and more effective) leaders who are keen to create positive impact for people and planet. Leaders who can see, feel and navigate the whole system with more ease and grace.

The Wise Leadership Universe model that I share with you focuses on your SELF, your STAKEHOLDERS and your SYSTEMS. By approaching each of these areas with a heightened awareness and the aim to more deeply connect with yourself, others and the environment, you are building a solid foundation of knowing what to care about, whom to care for and how to care. Ultimately, you take full responsibility and commit to deliver the best, most positive impact possible.

By practising the 'connect — care — commit' approach, you might find it easier to show up as your best, fully energised self. You simply can give more. When learning to better manage your own energy, you also realise where else energy awareness and management are important. You might see and feel more connections with other people and the surrounding systems, nature being a very important one. Becoming more aware of our connections to nature is vital.

While I am writing this final chapter, the COVID-19 pandemic is still sweeping around the globe. It is impacting every person — in either an economic, social or health-related way. The pandemic is also impacting the natural environment — positively and negatively. As people move around less and industries produce less, global CO_2-emissions have been reduced. At the same time, some governments use the distraction of COVID-19 to reduce protective environmental laws and regulations. At a local level, people who are bound to their houses and neighbourhoods start to rediscover what spending time in nature can do for them. They also start to notice all the things in their environments that they hadn't seen before. The positive things and the negative ones. We do not know yet what the sum of all these events will be for planet and people. It is a good reminder to lead and act from your circle of influence, while just keeping your circle of concern loosely in mind. Too much focus on events that you cannot change causes stress and does not get you anywhere.

A client recently told me that sustainability has moved further down the priority list of some of their stakeholders. Influencing them has become more challenging. Many people are in crisis mode and feel like they are just surviving. In an earlier chapter, we learned that by changing your perspective and mindset, you can move to a more thriving state where you can achieve a lot more with less struggle. This becomes easier when the whole community works together. Effective communication and collaboration increase your influence.

At the same time, there are leaders, like Leila Fourie and many others, who can see the opportunity in the challenges of the pandemic. My hope for you is that you are one of those realists. Many promote a variety of 'Green Recovery' projects. COVID-19 has acted like a magnifying glass — it has brought the things that weren't working to the forefront. This is where the world needs you to step up and do things even more effectively than you already are. You have got this!

There is little value in being a pessimist. Leaders get people moving and acting positively because they share hope. Doom and gloom make us passive. Luckily, change is a constant and there is always hope for something at least a little bit better. What you share and how you show up as a leader is your choice. My hope is that this book has given you some new perspectives, insights, tools and practices that will support you to be more naturally successful.

We need more leaders who improve the quality of life for everyone — not just for a few. Wise leaders who are naturally successful because they are highly energised, influential and impactful.

You are ready to join this group!

I can't wait to support you.

CONNECT WITH ME

As this is not yet the end ... where to from here?

Before you leave, let me say a big thank you for reading my book. I truly appreciate the time and energy that you have invested in considering my thoughts, stories and how-to processes. My hope for you is that you will get a great return on investment and become naturally successful beyond your wildest imaginings.

Books only ever convey a tiny part of the real world. They are a small part of the overall map of life. I'd like to show you more of the real beauty of the vast leadership landscape. I invite you to benefit from my twenty-five-years-plus experience in this field, combined with the insights I have gained from many unusual wisdom sources. Use me as your travel guide to create a smooth and safe trip for you and your team.

Check out my website www.ingridmessner.com, which gives you a brief overview of my services as mentor, coach, facilitator, trainer, speaker and author. You can sign up to my newsletter there.

If you'd like to have a chat about how you and your team can become more effective leaders, increasing your influence and positive impact, feel free to reach out to me directly.

I look forward to connecting with you.

Via email: ingrid@ingridmessner.com
Via LinkedIn: ingridmessner

Naturally yours,
Ingrid

REFERENCES / SOURCES

Chapter 1 — Self-Awareness

Study on self-awareness and success: Article 'New Study Shows Nice Guys Finish First'; published on website of American Management Association (2019). Available at: https://www.amanet.org/articles/new-study-shows-nice-guys-finish-first/

Steve Bradt (2010) 'Wandering Mind not a Happy Mind'. Published in The Harvard Gazette. Describing the research of Harvard psychologists Matthew A. Killingsworth and Daniel T. Gilbert. Available at https://news.harvard.edu/gazette/story/2010/11/wandering-mind-not-a-happy-mind/

Chapter 2 — Energy Management

Michael Bunn (2011): *Ancient Wisdom for Modern Health*. Enlightened Health Publishing.

Richard Barrett (2011): *The New Leadership Paradigm*. Lulu.com.

Tony Schwarz and Catherine McCarthy (2007): 'Manage your energy, not your time.' Harvard Business Review.

Mihaly Csikszentmihalyi (2008): *Flow: The Psychology of Optimal Experience*. Harper Perennial.

Dr. Kristin Neff on Self-compassion (2020): Resources available at www.self-compassion.org

Daniel Goleman and Peter Senge (2014): *The Triple Focus: A New Approach to Education.* More than Sound.

Ariana Huffington (2017): '10 years ago I collapsed from burn-out and exhaustion, and it's been the best thing that could have happened to me.' Published at Medium. Available at

https://medium.com/thrive-global/10-years-ago-i-collapsed-from-burnout-and-exhaustion-and-its-the-best-thing-that-could-have-b1409f16585d

Chapter 3 — Accountability

Peter Bregman (2016): 'The Right Way to Hold People Accountable.' Harvard Business Review. Available at

https://hbr.org/2016/01/the-right-way-to-hold-people-accountable

Patrick M. Lencioni (2002): *The Five Dysfunctions of a Team: A Leadership Fable.* Jossey-Bass.

Chapter 4 — Communication

Brené Brown (2018): *Dare to lead: Brave Work. Tough Conversations. Whole Hearts.* Ebury Publishing.

Patrick M. Lencioni (2002): *The Five Dysfunctions of a Team: A leadership Fable.* Jossey-Bass.

Matt Church (2019): *Rise up: An Evolution in Leadership.* Thought Leaders.

Stuart McMinn, Dharug Cultural Man (2020): Interview with Gone Bush Adventure available at https://www.youtube.com/watch?v=utcnaKM_9iw

Dr Sarah McKay (2016): 'The Myth of Multi-Tasking'. Published at https://drsarahmckay.com/the-myth-of-multi-tasking/

Oscar Trimboli (2019): *Deep Listening: Impact Beyond Words*. Oscar Trimboli.

Miriam-Rose Ungunmerr-Baumann (1988): 'Dadirri — Inner deep listening and quiet still awareness'. Available at https://www.miriamrosefoundation.org.au/about-dadirri

Erling Kagge (2018): *Silence: In the Age of Noise*. Viking.

Chapter 5 — Collaboration

Franz Metcalf and B.J. Gallagher (2018): *Being Buddha at Work*. Berrett-Koehler.

Buutzorg case study: Summarised from https://www.buurtzorg.com/about-us/. Inspired by Frederic Laloux's book: *Reinventing organisations*.

Gary Chapman and Paul White (2019): 'The 5 Languages of Appreciation in the Workplace: Empowering Organizations by Encouraging People'. International Journal of Offender Therapy.

Sarah McKay (2020), Neuroscience Academy, lesson 7.4. AIM — 'How to motivate others'.

Corey Moseley (2019): '7 Reasons Why Collaboration is Important'. Article published at https://blog.jostle.me/blog/why-collaboration-is-important

Paul J. Zak (2013): 'How Stories Change the Brain'. Greater Good Magazine. Available at

https://greatergood.berkeley.edu/article/item/how_stories_change_brain

Haeffel, G.J., Abramson, L.Y., Brazy, P.C. et al. 'Hopelessness Theory and the Approach System: Cognitive Vulnerability Predicts Decreases in Goal-Directed Behavior'. Cogn Ther Res 32, 281–290 (2008). Available at https://doi.org/10.1007/s10608-007-9160-z

Niki Harre (2018): *Psychology for a better world: Working with people to save the planet*. Auckland University Press.

Chapter 6 — Influence

Burwood Bricks & Living Building Challenge:

https://living-future.org.au/living-building-challenge/

https://www.burwoodbrickworks.shopping

Niki Harre (2018): *Psychology for a Better World: Working with People to Save the Planet*. Auckland University Press.

Jocelyn Davis (2019): *The Art of Quiet Influence: Timeless Wisdom for Leading Without Authority*. Nicholas Brealey Publishing.

Kerry Patterson, Joseph Grenny, David Maxfield, Ron McMillan and Al Switzler (2007): *Influencer — The Power to Change Anything*. McGraw-Hill Education.

James Clear (2020): *Atomic Habits*. Penguin Random House.

Chapter 7 — Context-Awareness

Max Dulumunmun Harrison (2012): *My People's Dreaming.* ReadHowYouWant.

Stephen R. Keller and Elizabeth F. Calabrese (2015): 'The Practice of Biophilic Design'. Available at https://www.biophilic-design.com

Terrapin Bright Green, LLC — various authors (2014): '14 Patterns of Biophilic Design — improving health & Well-Being in the Built Environment'. Available at http://www.terrapinbrightgreen.com/wp-content/uploads/2014/04/14-Patterns-of-Biophilic-Design-Terrapin-2014e.pdf

Clemens G. Arvay (2018): *The Biophilia Effect: A Scientific and Spiritual Exploration of the Healing Bond Between Humans and Nature.* Sounds True.

Waters Center for Systems Thinking (2020): Tools and strategies available at https://waterscenterst.org/systems-thinking-tools-and-strategies/tools-strategies/

Peter Senge (1994): *The Fifth Discipline: The Art and Practice of the Learning Organisation.* Doubleday.

Fridjof Capra and Pier Luigi Luisi (2014): *The Systems View of Life.* Cambridge University Press.

Donnella H. Meadows (2008): *Thinking in Systems.* Chelsea Green.

Sarah Cornally, Systems Constellation workshop, 18/8/16. More info at https://www.sarahcornally.com/meet-sarah/

David Snowden and Mary E. Boone (2007): 'A leaders' framework for decision making'. Cynefin model. Harvard Business Review.

Peter Senge (2020): 'There Are No Heroes: Peter Senge on System Leadership'. Interview. Available at http://leadership.mit.edu/no-heroes-peter-senge-system-leadership/

Chapter 8 — Stewardship

Quote by Dahr Jamail sourced from interview at https://www.lion-sroar.com/the-end-of-ice/

Kai Peters, Kurt April and Julia Kumar (2013): *Steward Leadership: A Maturational Perspective*. University of Cape Town Press.

Jane Goodall (2020): 'Humanity is finished if it fails to adapt after Covid-19'. Interview in The Guardian. Available at

https://www.theguardian.com/science/2020/jun/03/jane-goodall-humanity-is-finished-if-it-fails-to-adapt-after-covid-19?CMP=Share_iOSApp_Other

Yvon Chouinard (2016): *Let My People Go Surfing. The Education of a Reluctant Businessman*. Penguin.

Chapter 9 — Impact

Daniel Goleman, Peter Senge (2014): *The Triple Focus: A New Approach to Education*. More than Sound.

www.ingramcontent.com/pod-product-compliance
Lightning Source LLC
Chambersburg PA
CBHW040851210326
41597CB00029B/4801